sorry, we can't use funny

Barry Parham

ISBN: 145378618X
ISBN-13: 9781453786185
Library of Congress Control Number: 2010912872

Also by Barry Parham

Why I Hate Straws
An offbeat worldview of an offbeat world

Blush
Politics and other unnatural acts

What people are saying about *Sorry, We Can't Use Funny*

"Tightly written, with good timing and great delivery. So dry my cigarettes kept going out. Brilliant."

"This is certainly one of the best satire books I have read! Highly intelligent, very well thought through, and crafted with excellent writing skills."

"These stories bombard in a pleasant way, none of them failing."

"So funny and so clever!"

"What I love about this is not just the satire, that is as biting as it gets, but the myriad of writing styles that transcends the chapters ... splendid."

"You obviously have far too much IQ on your hands."

"I'm not gonna sit here and tell you how funny, great, quick, hilarious...I'm going to get back to reading it."

"Your voice is most distinctive and the humor in your writing is infectious."

"There has not been one chapter in this book that did not make me laugh out loud. Each chapter is a few minutes and I look forward to the next as I finish the one that I'm on. All have very different topics but are equally humorous. It's one of those sit-in-the-driveway-while-your-husband-goes-in-side-and-you-finish-the-chapter kind of books."

"I was reading Barry Parham's hilarious takes on life, love and the world we live in long before anyone else knew it was cool. So glad he's assembled this collection."

"Barry, you've done it again. Brilliant."

Dedication

This book is dedicated
to
Lila Grace & Claire

For short quips and long stares
For quick laughter and quiet wonder
For listening to jokes you don't understand
And loving me anyway

For letting me share this world through
your undimmed eyes

For granting me glimpses of God thanks
to your presence in this world

But most of all
For giving me

The best job in this world

Uncle Barry

Table of Contents

A Cultural Cul de Sac

General Relativity Motors

(Parallel parking in a parallel universe)

I own an invisible car.

I know. I understand your doubt. It was hard for me to believe, too. But it's the only thing left that makes sense. This many drivers can't all be out to get me, and they can't all be out of their minds.

Invisibility is the only remaining rational explanation.

It certainly makes more sense than trying to believe in some kind of coordinated, punitive pan-galactic anti-Me attack, or the sheer mathematical improbabilities required to support the existence of that many insane people.

Maybe it happens to you, too. You're driving along, at or under speed, in your own lane. You're not eating, or texting, or applying makeup. You're not contorting into the backseat to discipline misbehaving short people. Then, suddenly, off to the right, a grandmother launches her dust-streaked rice rocket right past that apparently optional, octagon-shaped red road sign, completely oblivious to you and your optics-challenged car. You shriek and slam on the brakes, just prior to soul-kissing her "I Heart My Grandkids" bumper sticker.

On other occasions, drivers ahead of me, who obviously can't see me, will just stop in the middle of the road. Just ... stop. Just brake, hold, pop a window and strike up a conversation with somebody in the adjacent yard, or the oncoming lane.

And then there's Testosterone Boy and his gothic date, The Attack Of The Mascara Monster, abruptly discharging their multi-story, metal-bar-enclosed, monster truck out of the Smoke 'N' Go parking lot, directly into the eyelashes of my headlights, causing me to emit extremely non-Sunday language.

Not that *that* helps. It does no good to yell. Remember - you're invisible. Now, you're wildly waving at passing clouds and birds, but the future felon just keeps on weaving down the road, checking in on his text messages, and checking out his young coed co-pilot with the sweater-threatening upper body assets. Now, you're in need of blood pressure meds, and Captain Freeway just keeps veering toward his mustard-stained destination at the Pile-O-Burger, totally angst-agnostic.

I think that's part of the problem: in our current culture, I have a relatively small car. I own one of the few remaining one-story motor vehicles on Earth. But then, I'm a Luddite on lots of levels. I have a cell phone that does nothing except make phone calls, if you can imagine such a foul, futile thing.

I'm still at sea about how the physics work out to support this potential invisibility phenomenon. There may be some car-park-particle versus road-rage-wave battle going on. Maybe my car is participating in some parallel existence-based, self-serving quantum pinhole experiment, as performed by the ancient Titans, or the neo-Republicans. Maybe my car is only visible within certain time-space-pavement parameters, only evident at the far points of some cosmic cul-de-sac continuum.

I bet Einstein would know. After all, Albert operated on a whole different level than the rest of us. Albert was out there. The guy saw time as a yo-yo, and space as a foldable Frisbee.

Here's how out there Einstein was. According to family accounts, Albert was slow to speak. He just didn't communicate as a small child – he simply spent his time walking around, looking around, occasionally teasing his hair.

Legend has it that young Albert never spoke until he was three or four years old, and that his first words were "this soup is cold." Later in life, when asked why he hadn't spoken pre-soup, Albert stared quizzically at his questioner for a second, finally replying, "Because, until then, nothing was wrong."

As they might say in recent public education standardized tests, that's just way cool.

If ever there was a thinker who drew Heaven's appreciative eye, here was that thinker. On a slow day, an Angel Third Class (Way Cool Science division) might have reviewed Albert's next-level notes and picked up the phone. "Not bad, Albert. Not bad. Hey, come 'ere. Watch this. I'm gonna make Edison's new phonograph say 'I buried Paul.' Wait for it ... wait for it..."

But meanwhile, back here on Earth, I need to figure out how to un-stealth my car, before somebody gets hurt. One day, I'm going to leave home to drive somewhere, and just "plink" out of existence, or arrive before I leave, or side-slide into some alternate universe where, for all time, I have to watch Hugh Grant movies.

Actually, my little Road Reality arcade game often begins before I ever even leave home. Sometimes I have a need to go to the grocery, I open the garage door, and some panel truck is blocking my driveway. Maybe my house is invisible, too. Heck, maybe *I'm* invisible. Maybe I really *have* gone where no man has gone before, and no, I don't mean to a Hugh Grant movie.

Well, enough about now and later for now, then. See you later.

And if you're *driving* when I see you, please return the favor.

The Curse of the Third Eye

(One of the benefits to self-analysis is I can validate my own parking)

Maybe it's just me.

Relatives, trying to be nice, tell me they would like to see my brain undergo a few tests. Nice people, nervously trying to edge toward the nearest exit, tell me I'm sick, but in a good way. Nervous people just walk away.

See, I have a condition. I'm either carrying around an extra gene, or missing one. I see and hear and watch the same things as you. But when I see and hear and watch them, I just seem to react differently.

Gift? Unlikely. Curse? Possibly. Covered by my health insurance plan? Hard to say.

Maybe it's just me. I'll let you judge. Witness:

While waiting in line to vote, I noticed a sign on the door at the school. The sign said "Please keep this door closed at all times."

At ALL times? Then why have a door?

Maybe it's just me.

I grabbed my pen and, just above the warning, scribbled "ENTRANCE TO HELL."

I watched a plane take off. It was branded "ValueJet." I don't know about you, but I don't want to fly with anybody named "ValueJet". I want to fly with "Fully-Funded Money-Flush Able-To-Afford-Multiply-Redundant-Maintenance-Crews Airlines."

When former comedian Al Franken was elected to Congress, all I could think about was sitting Senator Dianne Feinstein. Eventually, there's going to be a bill sponsored by them both. It's just a matter of time. I don't even care what the bill is about. I just want to hear them say it out loud: the Franken-Feinstein bill.

A home improvement store's ad offered this painting advice: "For 2 coats, double the amount of paint." You know, you just have to admire professionals at work. What a staggering display of mathematical acumen. And they shared such clever insights with us, the little people!

A Facebook user alerted the world that she was making chicken salad, and that she "broke down 2 chickens." She broke down two chickens? Does PETA know about this barnyard abuse? Were the chickens waterboarded? Were they even Mirandized?

A local TV station was updating the community on snowstorm-based church closings. According to the crackerjack typists at the station, there was a church somewhere nearby called St. Martyer.

Imagine - an entire religious sect dedicated to turning people into Ernest Borgnine.

At work, someone working on a project asked if they could import existing sites. "No," I told them. "You can only import sites that don't exist."

Maybe it's just me.

During a heated televised debate in Texas, some genius pointed out that if we make pot legal, that would cut down on the illegal use of pot. Clever lad. You know, if we make murder legal, that might very well reduce the number of arrests for murder.

A business owner told me he never comes in before 11.30am. So one day, I called him at noon. A staffer answered.

"He doesn't come in until 11.30."

"Okay. I'll call back in an hour earlier than now."

"Okay. Thanks, and have a nice day."

While installing some software, the next screen in the software wizard proclaimed, "Please press 'Finish' to continue."

Continue? Then we're not really finished yet, are we, darling?

A small store in my home town offered this marketing tease: "Ears Pierced While You Wait!" Well, HOW ELSE? What are we supposed to do, drop off our ears and come back later?

[EW] Hi, and thanks for calling Ear World!

[Me] What?

[EW] This is Ear World. Can I help you?

[Me] WHAT?

[EW] THIS IS EAR WORLD!

[Me] Are my ears ready?

[EW] What?

[Me] WHAT?

[EW] Sir, this is not funny.

[Me] I don't HAVE a bunny.

[EW] What?

I don't know. Maybe it's just me.

23

(Tonight on Phlox, an all-new episode of '23!' New day, new disaster, new American Hero)

11:00am

In America, a calm, clear day begins.

President Obama, acutely aware of his surprise Peace Prize, signs an executive order dismantling all military bases in Republican-leaning states. White House Tap Dancer Robert Gibbs points out the potential savings to Health Care.

At the troubled Counter Terrorism Unit, troubled agent Jack Bauer sits at a troubled computer terminal. Distracted by flagging ratings, he flips the wrong switch and inadvertently cancels his own show. Keifer Sutherland responds by waterboarding a Christmas tree.

Fox & Friends smoothly segues from "How To Bowl While Wearing Stilts" to "Dogs Who Can Bark The National Anthem."

Colorado citizens phone in sightings of a giant Jiffy-Pop-shaped spaceship.

12:00pm

In a shady credit default swap, Jack Bauer is rolled in reams of bogus mortgages and sold to a Chinese collector of Cleopatra memorabilia.

Foreign news wires and US intelligence confirm an uptick in al Qaeda chatter.

CIA transcript: Get me the translators. Did they say *jiffy-pop?*

1:00pm

Midwest news stations report that a homemade balloon, possibly carrying a small child, has escaped into the skies near Denver.

Fox & Friends smoothly segues from "Five-Minute Meals Made From Popcorn And Expired Milk" to "Why Not To Have A Vasectomy On A Ski-Lift."

2:00pm

Intercepted internet chatter hints that the balloon is actually an al Qaeda drone.

Alerted by the CIA to the balloon incident, the Air Force scrambles fighter jets in Colorado.

CIA transcript: Get me the Atlanta Bureau. Did they say *Falcon?*

3:00pm

Diverted by the balloon alert, NORAD overlooks an al Qaeda militia, invading Montana from the north. The terrorists are immediately repelled by six heavily-armed dermatologists on an elk-hunting junket.

Colorado citizens phone in sightings of a giant foil-covered mushroom cap.

4:00pm

Sheriff Joe Arpaio invades Colorado and arrests the ghost of Hunter S. Thompson, who is floating above Denver, trying to smoke the giant mushroom.

5:00pm

Fox & Friends smoothly segues from "Great Moments In Public Gargling" to "The Safest Cars That Weigh Under 20 Pounds."

Colorado citizens phone in sightings of a giant foil-covered Brussels sprout.

6:00pm

The balloon has not crossed state lines, so Congress can't interfere. But eager to participate in any hot-air event this close to an election year, Congress institutes a nuclear gerrymander, redistricting Denver as a Democratic precinct of Kansas.

7:00pm

President Obama, in order to squelch Sean Hannity and Bill O'Reilly, signs an executive order, the "Leap Hour Initiative," a mandate that permanently removes 8:00pm from time itself. Spokesman Robert "The Dreidel" Gibbs misquotes Chairman Mao, reminding reporters that "the great leap forward, the timid fall back."

9:00pm

The re-routed al Qaeda militia skirts Chicago, captures Indianapolis, takes a look around, and then gives it back.

10:00pm

FoxNews breaks a story: Boy Not Found In Balloon. For those just tuning in, this may be the single most useless headline ever uttered.

Not to be outdone, CNN breaks a story: Beef Not Found In Chicken.

11:00pm

Laid-off members of the Michigan National Guard queue up for Cash for Clunkers discounts.

A dispirited al Qaeda militia invades downtown Detroit, stocks up on poppy products, forms a pick-up team which handily defeats the Lions, regroups, and heads south.

Geraldo breaks a story: Chicken Not Found In Aruba.

12:00am

Obama flies to New Orleans, where he wins the Al Hirt trumpet competition and the Delta Queen beauty contest.

MSNBC notes that Obama did not take Air Force One to New Orleans: he just ... flew.

Fox & Friends smoothly segues from "Children Who Spontaneously Exploded During Natural Childbirth" to "Forty Ways To Serve Cheap, Tepid Wine While Re-Grouting Bathroom Tile."

1:00am

A southern flank of the al Qaeda militia invades New Orleans, Kansas Republicans invade Denver, and the governor of South Carolina invades Argentina.

2:00am

David Letterman vows to publicly out-apologize the governor of South Carolina.

3:00am

An all-male college announces a crack-down on cross-dressing. This isn't relevant, but it's still funny. One day, when you write your own story, you can opt for 'relevant.' Besides, it's 3am. Why are you still up?

4:00am

The combined al Qaeda forces converge on the Deep South. Accents on both sides suffer severe casualties.

CIA transcript: Did they say *all y'all* or *Allah y'all?*

5:00am

Colorado citizens phone in sightings of crop circles, which turn out to be tire tracks from the balloon recovery team. Sheriff Arpaio races in and arrests the crop circles.

6:00am

The al Qaeda troops pause for morning prayers and are instantly routed by the ACLU, who simply won't stand for it.

7:00am

Fox & Friends smoothly segues from "How To Caulk A Window In A Moving Vehicle" to "Light Snacks For A Post-Nuclear Armageddon."

8:00am

Still confused about the whole "Leap Hour" thing, America's budget-savaged military sleeps in. Meanwhile, the al Qaeda invaders close in on the true heart of America: NASCAR.

9:00am

Obama appears in a cape and tights. He checks his teleprompters, cues the Klieg lights, holds up a wooden staff, and intones something in a hope-filled way. Suddenly, the combined al Qaeda corps drop their weapons and kneel.

Sean Hannity notes that the genuflecting Jihadists are all given an ACORN t-shirt and a Kansas voter registration card.

10:00am

America is saved from yet another Overseas Contingency Operation, even though the operation wasn't contingent. Or overseas.

Obama wins the Nobel War Prize, the Julia Child Look-Alike Contest, and Double Jeopardy.

And Fox & Friends smoothly segues from "American Unemployed Out-Pace American Casualties" to "Fashion Tips For Leap Hour."

A Comedy of Eros

(From pagan Rome to pajama-grams in only MM years)

Every year, in mid-February, guys do the dance. All across this great land that used to be ours, millions of American males nearly forget Valentine's Day, freak out, and then stampede the stores for flowers & candy, or power-troll the internet for prurient PJs & overdressed teddy bears.

And all because of three guys named Valentine.

How did this happen? Who *are* these three guys? And why February?

Somehow, at some point, February got this reputation as a month of romance, maybe because it's cold. Plus, football's gone and we're stuck with the wildly popular sport of bowling, where you almost *never* get to see any serious violence.

According to my exhaustive research, performed in-between today's Toyota recalls, St. Valentine's Day contains vestiges of both early Christian and ancient Roman traditions, alongside their other time-honored traditions, like hot-dish picnics and mass public executions.

Holiday Factoid: "vestiges" is the classical Greek plural of "vest."

On this topic, the Catholic Church appears a bit confused, as they admit to recognizing at least three different Saints, all named Valentine: Valentine, Valentinus, and Val Kilmer (starring Tom Hanks as Forrus Gumpus). All three men were martyred, one of the serious downsides of achieving Sainthoodedness. Coincidence or not, they all died during various Februarys, shortly after forgetting to buy a nice gift.

One legend describes Valentine as a pagan priest who paganized around Rome during the reign of Emperor Claudius II (spelled "too") in the Third Century (spelled "III").

Holiday Factoid: The Third Century actually went on for several hundred years, until some bright bulb finally invented "IV" (spelled "hospital feeding tube").

But on one particularly slow Ides, Claudius outlawed marriage for young men, based on his theory that single guys would be better soldiers, proving that Claudius had never met me. But Valentine continued to perform marriages in secret, until finally, on the Ides of February, around III-thirty, Claudius decreed that Valentine be - as the ancient Roman Navy Seals would put it - "martyred with extreme prejudice."

Some believe that the Christian church chose to celebrate Valentine's Feast Day in February in an effort to upstage the pagan Lupercalia festival (held on February Ides), a seriously wine-washed fertility fair dedicated to Faunus Corruptus (the Roman secretary of the Department of Agriculture), as well as to the founders of Rome, Aunt Romulus and Uncle Remus.

Holiday Factoid: "Ides" is the classical Greek plural of "Ide."

In ancient Rome, Spring officially sprang in February, and it was a time for purification rituals (they didn't like bowling any more than we do). Houses were ritually swept clean and then, paradoxically, fouled up again by sprinkling the floors with salt and a type of wheat, paradoxically spelt "spelt." Members of the Luperci, an order of Roman priests, would then gather at the sacred cave of Rome's famous twins, Romulan and Klingon, lob some spelt around the place, and sacrifice a goat (for fertility) and a dog (for purification) and, paradoxically, they did it all with a straight face.

Afterward, young Roman boys (the Luperkinder and the Crips) would slice the goat's hide into strips, dip the strips in sacrificial blood and then hit the streets, gently slapping women with the foul things. Rather than mace-blinding the little punk truants, Roman women actually welcomed these advances, because it was believed that getting smacked with pieces of a dead goat would somehow make them more fertile, a characteristic referred to by many anthropologists as "rock stupid."

I don't even want to know what they did with the dog.

Later in the day, all these bitterly desperate young women would place their names in a big urn. The city's less-picky bachelors would then pull a name out of the urn, and the couple would be legally paired for the next CCCLXV days, or until one of them got eaten in public by lions, whichever came first.

Holiday Factoid: I didn't have to make up anything in the previous IV paragraphs. And we wonder why aliens don't bother landing here.

Finally, around 498 AD, somebody figured out that whole "IV" thing, and the Third Century came to an end. To celebrate, Pope Gelasius ("Jelly Daddy") officially declared February XIV as St. Valentine's Day, and he hosted a huge Lupercalian "goat-strip & light hors d'oeuvres" social mixer. Sadly, the celebration soured when a Hun named Bugs Moran, who had forgotten to buy a nice gift, was massacred by Al Capone.

The first ever 'valentine' greeting may have been sent by Priest Valentine himself. While serving time for running around Rome marrying people, he himself fell in love - it may have been the jailor's daughter, Nihil Corsetus, or it may have been his cellmate, Lancet Maximus. According to legend, he wrote a letter to the apple of his I, which he signed 'From your Valentine,' an expression that is still used today, but not in prison.

Although written Valentines were rare until after the year IV-Teen-Hundred, oral Valentine greetings were popular as far back as the Middle Ages. These feudal felicitations were usually yelled back and forth across rutted roads filled with fetid mud, Monty Python plague-carts and abandoned goat strips. Hearty knaves would hail dainty damsels, ushering in the age of the wolf whistle: "Yon Hottie! Carest thou to hie hither to my place? Truly, thou art the bomb! Fuh sooth and shizzle!"

The first commercial Valentine's Day greeting cards in the U.S. were created in the 1840s by Esther A. Howland, using lace, ribbons and colorful pictures known as "scrap," and then sold at colorful prices known as "insane."

Holiday Factoid: "Esther A. Howland" can be rearranged to spell "Hot Snared Whale." Coincidence? I think not.

In America, over L percent of all Valentine's Day cards are purchased within II days of the day itself. One source claims that a billion Valentine cards are sent each year, while another source puts the number at 188 million, which tells me that both statistics are coming from the Congressional Budget Office.

Interestingly, 85 percent of all Valentine's Day cards are purchased by women. This is part of a sadistic, coordinated plot, hatched by the notorious FGB (Female Guilt Bombers), whose evil plan is to empty the shelves of cards, just before last call, just to spite all us last-minute losers.

And as us losers age, it gets even trickier. For every 100 single women in their 20s, there are 119 single guys, many of them unindicted. So, in that age bracket, our side can keep up with the shopping mandates. But for every 100 single women in their 60s, there are only 34 of us. Tricky. But then, thankfully, the bell curve begins to flatten: for every 100 single women over age 100, 100% of single guys are dead.

One more note - the average American consumes some 25.7 pounds of candy each year, which means that if St. Valentine, at fighting weight, were to get dipped in chocolate, six random Americans would actually eat him.

Holiday Factoid: There's a place in Texas called Loving County. There's also a Heart Butte in Montana, and with a name like "Heart Butte," I'm guessing they blow the bell curve on per capita candy consumption.

Ultimately, Valentine's Day, on several levels, is simply a tricky holiday for guys. Witness: I was walking through a store's Valentine's Day section when I spotted some "Nobody Else But You!" greeting cards. I thought, "What a nice confirmation of one's commitment!" And then I noticed.

The cards were sold in packs of six...

9 Out of 10 People Can't Be Right!

(Only 8 million more shopping ads till Christmas!)

Okay. Summer's over. Time to start getting ready for Christmas.

Or X-mas, or Winter Solstice, or whatever we're allowed to call it this year.

Already, at the grocery, they're piping in holiday tunes, timeless standards like "I'm Dreaming of a Melanin-Challenged Christmas," "Rudolph, the Mishandled-Socialist-Experiment-Nosed Ecologically-Threatened Forest Denizen" and "O Come, All Ye Randomly-Generated Human Lifeforms."

According to a recent poll, 96% of us believe in God. So, nearly 1 in 10 don't. This means that if you're at the grocery checkout, odds are that somebody in line thinks the Universe just popped up on some ancient Tuesday. Just popped up, from nothing.

By the way, this 'somebody' is easy to spot. It's the guy buying four cans of potted meat, a packet of machine screws, a box of Saltines, a battery, Oreos, six liters of mayonnaise and a light bulb.

But polls aside, some people still don't believe that believers believe what they believe. Meanwhile, atheists have just won the right to purchase advertising space on public buses. To advertise *what?* How do you advertise "nothing?" How's this:

You're just a cosmic error. Brought to you by We 'R' Us. Call 1-800 D-I-E A-L-O-N-E

Just close your eyes, click your heels together three times, and say, "There's no place!"

Atheism. Because who needs hope, love and eternal life?

Do polls confirm what we believe, or disclose what we want? What would have happened if Moses had taken a poll?

"Nation of Israel, behold the Ten Commandments! Okay, Ten Suggestions. Okay, let's vote."

"Sir?"

"Yes, B'ob?"

"About that whole 'covet' thing? Shirley al-Khansent and I probably ought to sit that one out."

So it's once again time to get busy on that holiday shopping list. But this year, it's going to be tough, shopping for friends and family, since Uncle Fed already gave everybody new cars, new appliances, free health care, and economy-stimulating walking trails. Hopefully, one of those handy walking trails is slated to span the US/Mexico border, so all those undocumented randomly-generated human life-forms can more quickly get in line for their new cars and free health care.

Thankfully, though, we've managed to sneak a peek at some "Letters to Santa" from various public figures, to help you pick out some thoughtful gifts:

Green Czar Van Jones, who isn't even green, asks Santa for a "History of Electronic Media" coloring book. For decades, apparently, Mr. Jones never noticed that people actually keep videotape, and can replay it on TV at the most inconvenient times.

Nancy Pelosi isn't green, either, though she usually sports the pained expression of someone who just ate something not quite ripe. She asks Santa to replace her worn-out "My First Gerrymandering Kit."

President Obama refuses to be limited to a list. If it popped up in the Universe on that primordial Tuesday, he wants it. So do the patriotic thing. Send him your stocking.

Arlen Specter has two stockings this year, and expects Santa to fill 'em both.

Sarah Palin has no gift requests, but threatens to dope-slap anybody else who mentions her stockings.

MSNBC asks Santa for one more viewer, so they'll have two.

Charlie Rangel, who was so busy writing laws to make us pay our taxes that he 'forgot' to pay his own, already got his present this year. The IRS, that universal icon of sympathy and forgiveness, charged him no interest or penalties. None. Nothing. "Oh, it's okay, Charlie. Nudge, nudge, wink, wink, eh? No big deal. Ha ha ha."

Hmmm. No penalties? Now that sounds like a miracle to me. Maybe there's some tru …

Nah.

So say 'so long' to summer! Be of good cheer, evolutionary blobs of random matter! And may you have a very Merry Ethno-Generic Fully Optional Deity-Nonspecific Seasonal Timespan!

Caught Between Woodstock And Wall Street

(1970. Restless youth. Clueless, too.)

"Does he really think that's attractive?"

Yep. I said it. And no sooner had I uttered the comment than the truth hit me. I had turned into my parents.

In this dodge-ball game we call "life in America," some things sneak up on you. And one day, you realize they've been hanging around for a while, and they've laid claim to a piece of your life and your lifestyle. Other things seem to just suddenly spirit in one morning and then won't leave. They don't grow on you, they bolt onto you.

I'm not sure which is worse. Doesn't matter. You're stuck with them. And now you've crossed that generational Rubicon. You've become your parents.

"Does he really think that's attractive?"

It was at the grocery when it happened. I saw a guy with piercings. I don't mean a few ear-studs, vertically stacked like coliseum concert amps. I mean bulk piercings, as if the guy had found some obscure precious metals tax loophole that guaranteed him cash rebates by the ounce. For a minute, I thought his face was some kind of interactive Connect-The-Dots game, provided by the grocers as a kiddie diversion. The guy looked like an android was trying to escape his head.

Things sure were different, back when my generation was changing the world.

I'm not exactly sure how our culture chronologically defines the term, but I grew up in what is fondly referred to as "back in the day." And back in the day, just like now, kids got bored. But not that bored. I never got so ennui-soaked as to suggest, "Hey, Billy! Let's go drill some holes in our heads!"

In fact, on the Radical-Fashion-Meter, we were unbelievably tame, though we thought differently at the time. In our imaginations, we were fringe. We were haute couture, with fangs. We were OUT there!

Here's how totally out-of-control we were, back in the day. We wore...are you ready?...we wore denim. In public! We wore denim jeans, which, at the time, was something that polite people changed OUT of before they presented themselves to civilized society.

It gets worse.

We wore denim jeans with – now, hang on to something - with flared legs. These were called "bell-bottoms."

Back in the day, bell-bottoms were radical to the point of heresy, and virtually guaranteed my generation a no-waiting, laminated uber-pass to Perdition itself.

To further impede the efforts of Big Bad Authority, some of us even bought pre-damaged denim: jeans intentionally marred with rips and holes and stains. Clever, huh? That'll show the "establishment," eh?

We wanted to rebel, we really did. We wanted to be outraged. We so desperately wanted our own cause. But then came the bad news: life was good. We didn't have the Viet Cong; we had Donkey Kong. We didn't have animus; we had an allowance.

What do you do, when you want to be bitter, and life *doesn't* suck?

We wore tie-dyed shirts (look it up). We wore insanely wide ties, often stamped with the American flag, or the head of Che Guevara. We painstakingly styled haircuts called the "mullet." No, naming a haircut after a flat fish didn't make sense. That was the point. I think.

In the interest of full disclosure, I admit that there's an extant 1970's photograph of me and a date, posing for the obligatory parental pre-prom photo. My date was gorgeous, and sane. I, on the other hand, showed up with the hair of a medieval barber. I looked like an electrocuted yak.

It gets worse.

I was sporting a bow-tie so broad that it had its own zip code. The Navy could've used it to launch an F-16. And I shamelessly appeared in a wide-lapel tuxedo, in a shade of pastel blue rarely found in even the most generous Crayon collection.

It gets worse.

It was a velour tuxedo.

For those of you under the age of 40, velour was a substance once substituted for actual clothing. It was a synthetic fabric with the texture of deep-pile carpet, all the class of a intestinal malfunction joke told in church, and the resale value of a half-empty Chernobyl sour cream container. But don't take my word for it; here's scientific proof. Only two man-made objects are visible from outer space: the Great Wall of China and robin's-egg-blue velour tuxedos.

"Be extremely subtle, even to the point of formlessness." So advised the Chinese warrior-philosopher Sun Tzu, over 20 centuries ago, in "The Art of War." And though I'm not up-to-speed on the importance of the senior prom in ancient Chinese history, I'm fairly certain they would have frowned upon outfitting their dynastic storm troopers in pale blue velour. (We'll discuss yak-like hairstyles some other time.)

Sadly, my generation had no such restrictive sense of shame. Apparently, we just wore stuff, simply because it was stuff nobody else had ever thought to wear.

And I won't even get into something we used to call "leisure suits." That would just be cruel. Some of you might be trying to eat.

But we were rebelling, and we were immortal. We thought we were that thing that was the best of all possible things: cool.

But then we went postal. We went bat-barking insane. I don't remember how it started; who thought of it first. Maybe it was Che Guevara. But it was an act of rebellion never imagined by history's most wild-eyed and restless, and it nearly undid several thousand years of social and cultural progress.

We, the fine young men of America, started parting our hair down the middle. Honestly. We did.

Did we really think that was attractive?

Forgive us, one day, if you can.

And then, while you're in that gentle mood, forgive us for disco, too.

A Creyer Christmas

(Small towns, big events, high holidays, low tolerances)

Here in my town of Creyer (pronounced "Cur"), everybody that's got central heat is excited about Christmas. The whole place is geared up, hunkered down, nestled in, and shopped out.

To be sure, it's colder than Tiger Woods' in-laws at an Olan Mills family photo shoot, but we're all glad to be home for the holidays. In Creyer, Christmas is a magical time.

Our mayor, Carl "Big Carl" Sweeney, owner of Big Carl's Funeral Parlor And Fireworks Emporium, has plugged in the spinning color wheel for the Court House Christmas tree, and the City Council stopped kissing babies long enough to re-approve the town's annual sales tax holiday on candy, dental implants, cordwood and guns.

Big Carl's twin girls, Euphoria and Carl's Junior, have taken up their traditional position out in front of the Sonic, wearing plus-sized red jumpers and odd little nurse hats, whacking a cowbell and collecting money for needy children unless they're needy north of Virginia. Euphoria wants to thank everyone for their generosity; Carl's Junior claims they've already filled up the donation spittoon several times.

Cecil Sawsill down at Cecil's Trough 'N Lube has caught the spirit: anybody who chips in for the twins' worthy cause gets a "Three-Bean Buffet and Air Bag Inspection" discount coupon. When time allows, Big Carl likes to pitch in, too, standing next to the twins and ho-ho-ho-ing away, all dressed up as Saint Nicholas, or as he's known around here, "Santy."

The Creyer Municipal City Opera & Back Hoe Repair Company wants to remind everyone not to miss this year's Christmas Eve special, "A Mormon Hanukkah," guest-starring Orrin Hatch as Yentl Ben.

Over at Cotton Mather Elementary, the Chaste Cherubs are wrapping up rehearsals for the Christmas Pageant, and we hear that glee club director Randy Leggins has a real corker planned. Among other holiday classics, the Cherubs will be acting out "The Ten Days of Christmas" with sock puppets.

Now, in your town, you're probably used to "The Twelve Days of Christmas." Not in Creyer. The Ladies' Auxiliary at the Charismatic Serpentarium pitched a fit till we cut that verse about nine ladies dancing. And the Creyer Saints of the Second Amendment allowed that "three hens" is fine, but they're not going to have respectable church-going children running around singing about France. Not at Christmas.

However, Tommy "Towhead" Grimes, owner of the "Grimes of Passion" adult boutique, ran his usual pre-Christmas ad in the Creyer newspaper, the *Literable Gazette*, showcasing his holiday line of red flannel French teddies.

Not a peep from the Saints.

Tyrell's Pole Dancing And Lunch Buffet added a nice, festive touch, dolling up all the dance poles to look like candy canes, and headliner Dentitia "Eveready" Devereax is hinting of a new "Naughty & Nice" number that aims to please. Towhead got a preview and called it a miracle.

That Dentitia is something else. A few decades back, you'll recall, she was declared a national treasure by the Singapore Bureau of Alternative Tourism. Over the years, Dentitia's gotten so much coal in her stockings that West Virginia offered to have her strip-mined.

As always, responsibility for setting up the city's manger scene fell to the good sisters at Our Ladies of Perpetual Gastritis. But it was mighty cold out, and they took to nipping at the cider. They barely managed to get Rudolph and the shepherds in place next to Pinocchio before the sisters were spotted on Pearl Street, jiggling along in a conga line.

Curlene Getwilder, Otto and Candy's "gifted" daughter, tried to replace one of the wise men with a life-size cutout of Mike Huckabee, but the good sisters spotted the switch almost immediately. Otto argued that Mike Huckabee was, too, a wise man, and way more sensibly dressed. Otto makes a good point.

And finally, Tookey Ankle, night manager at Pawpaw's Fine Jewelry And Bait Shop, invites any last-minute shoppers in for a peek at his animatronicated Fly-Fishing Elves display, featuring that stocking-stuffing favorite, the collapsible Christmas crèche creel. While you're in there, be sure to register for a free Donna Karan tackle box – now available in black or black!

So, from all of us in Creyer, we wish you a Merry Christmas. And whatever you do, don't forget the real reason for the season: January markdowns!

Noah Joins the AARP

(The advantages of growing older. This will be a very short article.)

Here's something you may not know. When you turn 50, you start getting some very interesting invitations, many of them legal.

To be sure, there are other fantastic advantages to growing old, like outbreaks of persistent eyebrow dandruff. I'm still a bit unclear as to the beneficial function of this particular bodily activity, but I'm someone who likes to believe that all things happen for a good reason, and that makes me stupid, which is another advantage to growing old.

But at the onset of age fifty, there's a sudden perverse and pervasive interest in you, from various parties that never bothered to speak to you before, or haven't noticed you since you were in your twenties and immortal. Once again, you've become a target audience to marketers, and not just manufacturers of anti-eyebrow-dandruff miracle creams. Of course, marketers can easily find you now, due to things like the IRS, the US Census, and the fact that you were stupid enough to tell the truth in your Facebook profile.

For example, when you hit 50, Facebook starts targeting dating ads at you. The ads make the dubious claim that, somewhere out there in cyber-land, there are teeming hordes of young women, with names like Minky and saddled with serious glandular imbalances, desperate to meet you. These in-your-face ads feature oddly-positioned young women who, quite frankly, look like they're smuggling traffic cones, and they're all staring at you while inordinately leaning forward, as if they'd just dropped something on the floor (probably your eyebrow dandruff elixir).

The eager young Minky, of course, can't appreciate that your current Sowing Of Wild Oats status is somewhere south of "clinical coma." Remember, you've hit that age where simply sleeping on a lumpy pillow will malform your entire spine for the next 72 hours.

At this age, you no longer worry about appearances - you worry about appliances. At this age, you no longer try to stay awake all night - you try to stay awake all day. At this age, you're too jaded to want to be immortal, and too tired to want to be immoral.

And then, of course, there's the AARP. When these staggeringly relentless maniacs discover you've hit the Bea Arthur milestone, they lurch into a printing/mailing frenzy that would shame Publisher's Clearing House. Before you can even blow out that 50th candle, the AARP are shipping you temporary membership cards, and you need to know that they will keep sending them, approximately every eleven minutes, until that post-formative day when your family, friends, and the IRS show up to comment on how natural you look, lying there in the penultimate parlor.

You can also look forward to being pleasantly mail-bombed by many of the planet's finer pharmaceutical companies, which for some reason all seem to be based in Canada, or former Russian republics. You can generally recognize the unsolicited emails from these entities by the screaming virus alerts that fire off when one of their 'buy now!' teasers show up in your e-mailbox. These helpful homeopaths automatically assume that, at your advanced age, you have surely succumbed to the standard set of age-based ailments: you know, loss of hearing, more trips to the 'reading room,' a mild inability to consistently make Minky levitate, etc.

And these invaders will practically *demand* that you let them help you with what, in my opinion, is the single nastiest word in the English language. I won't ruin your afternoon by using that word here, but it rhymes with "Swimmer Droids."

It gets better. You may be contacted by molded young sales professionals with wind-tunnel-proof hairdos and permanent lockjaw who would like you to consider a 'reverse mortgage.' As best as I can tell from my extensive research in the reading room, this is a clever arrangement in which you un-buy the house you've worked your whole life to buy. Apparently, if you manage the timing just right, you can arrange to be Potter's Field fodder exactly 30 seconds before Minky sues you and your estate, claiming "irreconcilable differences."

(Since time is limited – mine, not yours - I'll glide past the relentless mailings you'll inevitably receive from funeral homes, graveyards, crematoria, and pro-choice groups telling you that it's never too late to abort yourself.)

"Old," of course, is a relative term, unless you're an older relative. According to the Bible, people used to live much longer than we do now. Or maybe, given some of the stories I've read about life during the Old Testament, life just *seemed* longer.

Imagine it. You're Noah. You're 945 years old. You've memorized every tired rerun on CBS (Central Broadcasting Scroll). Your eyebrow dandruff is flaring up. You're still recovering from that whole Ark episode, you've been hanging up on persistent AARP marketers for over 7 centuries, and you've got Pharisees crawling all over you about fathering a child with Minky when you were old enough to, well, to know better. Prophets and seers are running about, making snide Strom Thurmond comparisons. And if that weren't enough, you may need to visit the red tent to get some advice on Swimmer Droids. You decide to duck out for a quick nosh.

But then that nudnik, Methuselah, the deep-fry guy and counter clerk at Baal Burger, cards you before honoring your Senior Discount.

And now you know what finally killed Methuselah.

Sorry, We Can't Use Funny

(Facing the Fourth Estate, the Fifth Dimension, and some serious candle management)

About a year ago, I wrote a book. I didn't mean to. I had to.

There was no other choice. I had to do it. Somehow, I had managed to snub a minor deity, and I had to set things right.

True, I did want to write. Always have. But not a book. I don't have what it takes to write a novel. I'm missing a few of the essentials: a plot, a plan, an intimate relationship with a bunch of interesting characters, vocabulary, discipline, etc. But enough about my personal life.

I wanted to write something less dramatic, something more useless, something that lets me get away with gross grammatical gaffes like, for example, the previous paragraph. I wanted to write a weekly "look-around-and-comment" piece, and then try to find some newspaper willing to carry it, so I could get out of the numbing habit of actually working.

And so, for a while, I tried to do just that - writing stuff and contacting newspapers all across America. But the newspapers kept telling me to get out of the way so they could finish dying.

Like every other industry that hasn't yet been bought by our government (or sold to the Chinese one), newspapers are struggling. I soon realized that I'd picked the worst possible time in 3 decades to ask newspapers to spend money they didn't have to spend, or just didn't have.

So it didn't go well, and now I focus on writing other things, shorter things: online columns, internet articles, pay-per-view short stories, long parole violation rationalizations, extended grocery shopping lists.

Everywhere I go, thousands of people stop me and ask, "Where do you come up with these ideas?" (Okay, not thousands. My parents ask. And a close friend, who reads my columns and is concerned, asks. And, for some reason, one weird guy who is always curled up just outside the door at the grocery, deep in conversation with invisible minor deities.)

But the answer is simple. When trolling for column ideas, I have several things working in my favor:

- My television has a functioning "on" button.
- I haven't bothered with actual facts since the Nixon Administration.
- I have constant access to Earth, known throughout the Milky Way as "That Weird Blue Planet With All Those Gods."

Did you know that, on parts of our planet, people have to keep up with some 300 million deities? That's some serious specialization. Imagine trying to remember who handles what, whose bell is whose, which candle is which, who's been acknowledged already today and who hasn't. Undoubtedly, some minor deities are bound to get snubbed, here and there, now and again.

300 million. Hard to imagine. Even in our own Congress there are only 535 deities. And none of them are actually omnipotent – they just act that way. And of course, *they* snub *us*.

So the challenge is not in finding writing material. The challenge is writing fast enough to keep up with it all. For example, while working on this column, the following headlines yelled at me from the TV:

- Cat Obesity Is On The Rise
- Feds Impose Strict Standards On Things Sold At Garage Sales
- Nancy Pelosi Calls Health Care Bill A "Christmas Present To America"

I rest my case.

But I still couldn't find any takers in the print media, maybe because I had inadvertently intoned to the wrong minor deity, or snubbed the relevant one. Maybe I had lit a candle to the one in charge of Car & Driver, Holiday Editions, Back-Issues Only. Mistakes can happen. With a staff directory of 300 million, it's easy to end up in the wrong cubicle.

When the newspapers responded at all, responses ranged from "No thanks" to "Nice stuff, but we're broke" to "I write all our humor, thank you" to "We only use local writers, but if you move to Bean Blister, Idaho, call me!" to my very favorite: "Sorry, we can't use funny."

Then, one day, I read an article that suggested something new: Why not pay buckets of money to publish a book, and then include a free copy when you contact comatose, near-death newspapers? That way, you'll not only be snubbed - you'll be broke, too!

Hard to argue with logic like that.

So I wrote a book. Bad idea. Because now I couldn't help myself. Now I wanted to *sell* the book. How hard could *that* be, right?

Turns out that over 500,000 book-shaped things are published, every year, or about one book for every 600 minor deities.

Turns out that the average author sells a whopping 250 copies of her/his book, unless the book describes a new diet, or discusses all 300 million minor deities, or outlines how you didn't kill your ex-wife, but if you had done it, which you didn't, here's how you would have done it, which you didn't.

Regardless, I wrote and published a book, listed it online, and tackled the task of trying to actually sell it. Counting my parents, I could be sure of selling two copies. Adding my close friend, I could be sure of selling ... uh ... two. And I had no idea what the guy outside the grocery liked to read.

Time passed. Sales inchwormed along. I remember the day when I cracked the ceiling - the day that my stories and I earned our very first dollar. Top o' the world, Ma! I immediately broke out a picture of a bottle of champagne. I lit a little candle to the minor deity in charge of Online Paperback Books, 250 Pages Or Less, Sales Of Exactly One Dollar (deity 12,615,411, if you're wondering). I opened a magazine to a photo of rich people, and stared at them, memorizing faces for future reference. I was lost in the reverie. I stared at my new friends for so long that I developed an ocular tic, and had to schedule with the eye doctor.

A whole dollar! As I leaped into this new tax bracket, with my one good eye, I knew I had to readjust for such staggering wealth. Maybe it was time to consider a down-payment on a new hat. I instructed my broker to begin investing heavily, maybe go long on re-usable minor deity candles.

I know that one single dollar is, well, nothing. But annualized? Well now, that's ... that's ... well, that's *still* nothing. But then, one day, things began to bubble up. According to the online "sales rank," my little book was the 256,609th most popular book in America, just ahead of "How I Lost

50 Pounds And Partial Eyesight By Eating Pictures Of Food" and just behind "Harry Potter And The Curse Of A Whole Bunch Of Snubbed Minor Deities."

So, naturally, I went insane. I started checking the online sales rank every 11 seconds. And my book rose and fell within those sales rank numbers, bobbing and weaving like a minor deity jockeying for position on the prayer shelf.

Should you ever publish a book, here's a little Rookie Writer Sanity Tip: don't check your online sales rank every 11 seconds. During one day, my book's ranking dervished from 30,000th place, up to 15,000, then 9,000, back down to 12,000, back up to 6,000, and back to 20,000. Apparently, every hour of the day, thousands of people are busily writing books, and then un-writing them.

And I plan to start writing another book as soon as my eyesight returns. I'm just back from the eye doctor and need a while to, literally, re-focus. I'm so dilated right now, I may go into labor.

By the way, here's the working title for new book: *The 'I Didn't Snub My Ex-Wife's Minor Deities, But If I Had, Here's How I Would Have Done It' Diet.*

The perfect gift! Order your 300 million copies today!

People. They just can’t self-help it.

Abby Redux

(Free advice. It's worth every penny.)

Dear Abby Redux,

I'm told that life is hard, I'm owed nothing, I have to work for a living, things won't always go my way, and I may actually have to make my own house payments. Is this still America?

Signed,

Numbed By Entitlement

Dear Numbed By Entitlement,

Shut up.

Dear Abby Redux,

All my life, I've played by the rules. But in the last 200 days, I've lost my job, my investments, my home, my car, my credit, and my wife left me for another woman. At this point, I'm seriously thinking about moving to Mexico and then sneaking back in.

Signed,

On The Edge

Dear On The Edge,

Look on the bright side. At least the government still has your health.

Dear Abby Redux,

Is it just me, or does it seem like terrorist attacks by religious radicals are on the rise?

Signed,

Minimally Observant

Dear Minimally Observant,

Shame on you. Simply because 100% of recent terrorist attacks have been initiated by religious radicals, you stretch logic by assuming any kind of spurious pattern. That would be like saying that a bank was robbed by 4 guys wearing clown masks, the robbers were seen leaving the scene in a brown Ford Bronco, and then an overly reactive local police force put out an All Points Bulletin for 4 clowns in a brown Ford Bronco. I mean, really.

Dear Abby Redux,

I can't believe Sparkle was thrown off the "Survivor" island!

Signed,

Dismayed

Dear Dismayed,

I'm guessing you're the type of person who pays good money for two phone lines, just so you can vote twice during "American Idol." I would say "get a life" but I'm afraid you'd think it's some sort of self-help diet, or a new version of Windows.

Dear Abby Redux,

After President Bush signed the law that created Hurricane Katrina, I found myself with no home and no television. I moved into a cardboard box on the Louisiana coast and managed to eke out a living selling shrimp to a shifty-looking franchiser named Captain D. Yesterday, President Obama showed up on our beach and walked around in his shirt-sleeves, nodding knowingly. Then a nondescript bus showed up, 200 BP employees surrounded the President, and they all performed some kind of weird interpretive dance. Anything going on in the news I should know about?

Signed,
Percy Walker

Dear Percy Walker,

Not to worry. BP is currently performing a non-invasive deep-sea experiment, involving hemisphere-wide baths of potentially toxic chemicals in amounts that would kill a Klingon. BP's plan, assuming they ever actually get one, will result in mutant shrimp the size of a Neville Brothers' family reunion guest list, not to mention a very nice 3rd Quarter dividend for BP investors. Though it's hardly worth mentioning, there is a slight chance that these next-generation shrimp will be self-aware, heavily (and literally) armed, and have an in-your-face, anti-human attitude. Not to worry.

Dear Abby Redux,

I'm a soon-to-retire Home Economics teacher, and I'm not really familiar with new technology. My students keep talking about something called a "Facebook." What is a Facebook?

Signed,

Luddite

Dear Luddite,

Facebook is a digital diuretic. It's a social media website on the internet (still with me, sweetie?) where people go to share intimate details with friends they never met. On Facebook, you can keep up with captivating information, like this little time-lapse sample:

- Joey has 2 work today. Ugh.
- Joey is about to leave for werk. RU?
- Joey is leaving 4 work.
- Joey is on the way 2 work.
- Joey is almost @ work lol.
- Joey is at wurk.
- Joey hates work roflmao.
- Bitsy likes this.

Dear Abby Redux,

I'm a happily married, non-medicated, employed, Christian adult male, with pleasant children, a fondness for reading, no criminal record and no outstanding debt. Is there something wrong with me?

Signed,

Sleeps Well At Night

Dear Sleeps Well At Night,

Big yawn. Haven't you heard? Neurotically dysfunctional is the new black. I suppose you also volunteer, donate to charities, and believe in personal responsibility. These days, normal is, well, abnormal. Step up and self-loathe! Go get you some issues, man!

Dear Abby Redux,

What's with all this Right-Wing Conspiracy hate speech about President Obama tampering with elections? That can't be true, can it? I mean, look at that profile! And have you ever seen him nod knowingly?

Signed,

Crushed

Dear Crushed,

All is well. Before Obama was even born, George Bush dressed up like Rahm Emmanuel and instructed the ghost of Millard Fillmore to talk Joe Sestak out of running for the Senate. In return, Sestak was promised Arlen Specter's loyalty, which clearly is an object with no intrinsic value.

Dearest Abby Redux,

I am the prince of a smalling African nation, whose father was imposed in a more-or-less bloodless coupe, leaving me in charge of 28 millions of America's dollars sterling. I am unstructed by my finances advisory to place this funds in your personal bank of account, if you will only but to have leaving me your email address, and a valid card of credit number, replete with your secreted Personal PIN Identity Numbering. Largely do I look forward to our hearing from you at or near your earliest incontinence.

Signed,

An Anomalous Friend

Dear An Anomalous Friend,

Can't help ya, chum. I bought into that whole "government health care will save you money" scam, so, for the moment, I'm all suckered out.

Dear Abby Redux,

Maybe it's just me, but it sure seems like we lost something valuable when we stopped caring for each other. After all, the best things in life ... aren't things.

Signed,

Wistful

Dear Wistful,

My staff and I, your family and friends, and everybody reading this, all look forward to your leap into the current century. Catch up, putz.

Dear Abby Redux,

I wrote a book, and my Mom wants to buy a copy, but she won't let me give her a discount. She insists on paying full price.

Signed,

Guilty Conscience

Dear Guilty Conscience,

Shut up.

Dear Abby Redux,

My son wrote a book, and he expects me to pay full retail for it. After everything I've done for him!

Signed,

Maternal Guilt-Slinger

Dear Maternal Guilt-Slinger,

Shut up.

Dear Abby Redux,

I'm thoroughly insulted by those jack-booted thugs in Arizona who want to insist that illegal immigrants have immigrated illegally. And I'm putting my money where my mouth is. I'm boycotting everything Arizona-related, including cactus, retired people, that "Raising Arizona" movie, and Arizona Iced Tea. You with me?

Signed,

Outraged

Dear Outraged,

Arizona Iced Tea is made in New York state, you gullible knee-jerk knucklehead. You really should meet my friend, the African prince. What's your personally email?

Dear Abby Redux,

My husband is the former President of a certain country which, for understandable reasons of anonymity, I'll withhold. I recently came into possession of candid photographs, catching him yet again in a compromising position with a certain self-help columnist who publishes under the byline "Dear Abby Redux." Would you care to make a financial contribution to my next Presidential campaign?

Signed,

Secretary Of Something

Dear Secretary Of Something,

That all depends on what the meaning of "here my check is" is.

Bar(code) Hopping

(Odysseus and Einstein meet Enya and expired coupons)

Despite what you might think, the most brutal social equalizer in America is the not the Department of Motor Vehicles. It's the neighborhood grocery.

Sure, you might argue that the more likely candidate is the DMV. That's a fair call, but there are three problems with that analysis:

1) Not everybody drives, so not everybody has to visit the DMV.
2) We all have to buy milk. I think there's a law.
3) The DMV is not, technically, staffed with earthlings.

Yes, the grocery. And I'm not talking about those clever, trendy Mom 'n' Pop boutiques that sell eleven things (three are actually in stock), at prices that require a co-signer, and that employ piped-in Enya albums to discourage browsers. Granted, these boutiques are the be-and-end-all when your sadistic recipe calls for a half-bottle's spritz of non-necrotic, fully-fleece-friendly, free-range Azerbaijanian goat appendix. But we're not likely to long for such culinary treats here in America, where the average grocery list revolves around various types of cheese spelled with a "Z."

No, I'm talking about those cavernous shopping-center anchor stores with consistently misspelled names, like Bi-Now and Banana Republix and Kroakers and Great Big Honkin' Food Planet.

Admittedly, we could chat and dicker for days about the various irritations that define the grocery shopping experience. There are no clocks. There are no windows. There are 38 dozen check-out lanes (three are actually open). There are more "breakfast power bar" options than there are humans who can actually afford to eat breakfast. They have a bizarre fascination for magazines about miracle diets, Oprah, alien babies and Brad Pitt. To get from hamburger meat to hamburger buns requires 3 bus transfers and an estimated 2 hours (estimated, for there are no clocks).

Not to mention the subway ride back over to the grocery's Cheez Aisle.

But today, I want to draw your attention to the "check your own self out" lanes: those 4-6 little automated kiosks, off to the side, that theoretically let you warp-speed your way through the check-out process by theoretically scanning your own grocery items, with absolutely no human intervention whatsoever. It was, as polite people might put it, a "nice idea."

You know 'em. You wanna like 'em. You wanna use 'em.

You can't.

First, your ears are sand-blasted by some quasi-robotic female voice, welcoming you to the "your own self" process, and thanking you in advance for using the "your own self" process. I call her Gladys, after the legendary Greek Harpy "Calaeno," because I can't spell "Calaeno," and because I seriously doubt any dedicated scholars of ancient Greece are studiously hunched over this article, fact-checking my facts about check-out lines at the grocery.

Gladys then proceeds to lure your shopping cart in-between a pair of monsters, Scylla and Charybdis.

Okay, not true. Gladys does no such thing. According to Greek legend, Scylla had six heads, twelve feet, and dog heads coming out of her torso, and as such, she's not likely to be working at a local grocery, unless she belongs to a union. But again, I'm gonna run with the imagery until an alert Greek scholar pops in to call me on it, which is not likely to happen anytime soon, given that Greece seems to be busy trying to invade itself.

(Historical footnote: Scylla's partner in crime, Charybdis, was allegedly just a great big mouth that belched whirlpools three times a day, and is currently polling several points ahead in the 2010 Senate race in Nevada.)

Next, Gladys' robo-programming requires her to ask if you have any coupons or a <insert misspelled store name> frequent shopper card. This heralds your first actual interaction with "The Scanner" (starring Keanu Reeves as "Neo-Politan" and Adam Sandler as "Glitch").

Assuming you successfully scan your cards and coupons, or manage to convince Gladys and Senator Charybdis that you don't have any, you're then prompted to begin scanning the now-rancid food that you hauled up to "your own self" earlier that day. Gladys instructs you to scan your items and to immediately place them in one of the conveniently-located plastic bags, which were conveniently injection-molded into some kind of formless synthetic blob with no visible top, bottom, sides or openings. Note that you will have approximately eleven seconds to get each item into a bag before Gladys robotically sighs, raises her voice, and testily repeats her demand.

And, to be fair, the process works. For a while. But there's always at least one rogue grocery item that refuses to be scanned. Always. What to do? Sure, there may be a Certified Your-Own-Self customer service attendant standing nearby, sporting back-of-the-crayon-box-painted fingernails and busily text-messaging. So help is on the way!

Don't hold your breath. If there is actually an attendant on duty at all, she'll be harboring deep career resentments, silently blaming you for many things, and she'll look like someone whose great-grandparents lost a cruel bet at Ellis Island.

But feat not, gentle reader. As always, I'm here for you. There are many alternative scanning techniques you can employ to tame that recalcitrant grocery item. Here are some of my favorites:

- The Dickens Slow Burn: inching your grocery item every-so-slowly past the scanner (think "glacier"), in case the scanner needs a few more hours to decode the barcode, or a little more time to complete its Bachelor of Scan Arts degree
- The Tolkien Dragon: raising and lowering the item while moving it slowly across the scanner window, like some undulating uber-mountain-worm, under the assumption that the Scanner Gods will ultimately discover its heritage
- The Escher Alter-Angle: making the assumption that the scanner window will ultimately find a favorable point-of-view, if you'll just dimensionally twist and contort the grocery item enough times
- The Einstein Time Warp: rapidly shoving your item back and forth, back and forth, back and forth, until the laws of "this week's special" relativity kick in, at which point the scanner complies and subtracts the cost of gravity from your bean dip
- The Lovecroft Retina Burn: determinedly holding the grocery item in front of the cursed scanner until the food has passed its expiration date, at which point the on-duty attendant becomes wracked with guilt and goes on break.

One of these techniques is guaranteed to work. Soon, you'll be happily dripping ice cream across the parking lot and, on your way home, frantically trying to think up ways to finish your carton of milk before "The Date."

And then you get home and realize you forgot to buy cereal.

Decalogue 2.0

(Announcing the new Ten Commandments upgrade! Now with less guilt!)

Recently, on Facebook, I made a comment about religion. Lesson learned. I won't be doing *that* again.

It seemed like a good idea at the time. I had just watched a debate between an atheist and (to use common parlance) a clueless, close-minded, non-scientific, deluded idiot. The atheist, named Christopher XXX, was clever and literate, and clearly had convictions. For example, he was apparently boycotting shampoo, and seems to have valiantly stuck with his anti-Prell protest since, roughly, the Crusades. At one point during the debate, his forelock fielded a question.

(I don't know Christopher XXX personally, but I bet that, as an atheist, it must really chap him when he contemplates the first six letters of his name.)

Anyway, after watching the debate, I thought up a new philosophic worldview, and wanted to share it with my 86,417 Facebook "friends," a group that includes forty people I actually know and three strangers who claim to be practicing vampires.

Looking back, it made sense. Looking back usually does make sense, unless you're driving, or trying to outrun a vampire. In those cases, you should not look back, but just focus on getting where you're going, after which you should immediately update us on Facebook. I'm sure that, somewhere on Facebook, there's a "One-Legged Vampires" fan page.

I called my new philosophy "Barry's Relatively Absolute Theology." The core tenet of being a BRAT is a simple one: nobody has a right to tell me what to do, but I have every right to tell you what to do. How sweet is *that*, eh? Plus, all the heavy metaphysical lifting has already been done, since the discovery that Original Sin was George Bush's fault.

As a BRAT, I was particularly well-suited for the next step in my project: upgrading the Ten Commandments. The "absolute" part ensures that the Commandments are universal, while the "relative" part ensures that they are only universal from *my* perspective; that *my* laws only apply to what *other* people do. Think of it as a mix of timeless self-centered dogma and current Congressional behavior.

Now, in keeping with the relative nature of my philosophy, it holds that different situations have differing realities, because I said so. So I realize the need to provide several sets of rules, unique for several situational sets, but binding within all possible behavioral buckets. And, like Christopher XXX, I have the nerve, and I have the time. Plus, I own a comb.

So, here are the bucket lists of candidate commandments, currently under review by a whole team of BRATs. Perhaps you'll disagree with our lists, or perhaps you have your own. We don't care. That's the whole point of being a BRAT.

Bucket I: Driving & Traveling

- Thou shalt not drive in the passing lane at speeds normally associated with funeral processions, or golf carts.
- Thou shalt not leave thy turn signal blinking for 217 consecutive cubits.
- Thou shalt not attempt to board a plane with thy carry-on bag that is approximately the size of Lake Michigan.
- Thou shalt not drive a moped on public streets. For it is written: nay, thou dost not, in fact, own yon whole stinkin' road.
- When waiting for the light to change, thou shalt not explore the depths of thy nasal cavities.
- Thou shalt not borrow my car, tune the radio to the "Extremely Angry Grunge Band" station, and leave the volume set at "Attack of the Decibel Monster."
- Get off thy cell phone.

Bucket II: Media & Marketing

- Thou shalt not keep saying stuff is "absolutely free! you just pay shipping!"
- Thou shalt stop selling hot dogs in packs of 10 and hot dog buns in packs of 8.

- Thou shalt get it through thy thick heads that very few of us are concerned about our daily intake of bifidus regularis.
- Thou shalt never again say "I just wanted to reach out to you" with a straight face.
- Thou shalt cut it out already with the "please listen carefully, for our menu options have changed" declarations. Nobody's sitting at home thinking, "Six! Whaddaya mean, six? Last time your useless software crashed, I pressed eight!"
- Thou shalt stop screaming "Fox News Alert" when thy next news story is some lame fluff piece about cat obesity.
- Get off my cell phone.

Bucket III: Consumers & Coworkers

- Thou shalt not send me an email, then call me to ask, "did you get my email?"
- Thou shalt not sneak more than 10 items through yon "10 items or less" lane. Ten meanest ten. If I promised ten Commandments, then presented thee with twenty-six, thou wouldst not appreciate it, wouldst thou?
- Thou shalt absolutely stop using "interface" as a verb. And "incentivize." And "efforting." Stop it.
- Thou shalt not act like you're the first person in the history of grocery shopping to write a check. Nor shalt thou wait till the last possible second to begin scrabbling around in your Lake Michigan-sized purse for exact change.

- When at thy favorite fast-food franchise, thou shalt decide what thee wants to eat *before* walking up to yon counter.
- Turn down thy cell phone.

Bucket IV: Congress & Other Cathouses

- Thou shalt not take a cell phone call in the middle of a citizen's question, you rude, condescending ego-zeppelin.
- Thou shalt keep thy nose out of our business. On personal issues, such as how much our kids weigh, thou shalt shut up.
- Thou shalt stop asking to be re-elected so thee can fight for term limits.
- Thou shalt not "save" the economy, or education, or banking, or health care, nor shalt thou dance on the head of a pin, because thou so hast not a clue how stuff really works out here. Get over thyself.
- The next time thou actest like a rude, condescending ego-zeppelin, thou shalt immediately explode into 23 bukukillion pieces. We hopest.

Bucket V: Family & Friends

- Thou shalt not pirate DVDs, or remove that little "Do Not Remove" tag from your mattress.
- Thou shalt not almost, but not quite, finish the milk and then leave yon carton in yon fridge. If I catch you doing this, I *will* bust thee up.
- Dude. Thou shalt not, like, use, like, "like" and stuff as every other, like, word in your, like, sentence.

Obviously, thy public education system has let thee down.

- Honor thy parents for the rest of this year. Beginning next year, honor thy government nanny.
- When thou meetest thy foe on the field of battle, and thou art behind by 14, and thy foe is clearly showing blitz, thou shalt not send forth thy tight end on a deep slant pattern.
- Thou shalt not slam the screen door, for verily, thy parents-slash-government nanny brought thee up better than that. Wast thou raised in a barn?

By the way: if you run into Christopher XXX, please don't refer to him as Christopher Thirty. But feel free to call him X-opher. He'll love that.

Abby Redux II

(Abby fends off academia, alchemy and atavism)

Dear Abby Redux,

Do you think White House spokesman Robert Gibbs realizes how many times he says "obviously" during a press conference?

Signed,

Obviously Works From Home

Dear Obviously,

Obviously not.

Dear Abby Redux,

According to my coach, I have to take a philosophy class. According to a book I'm almost reading: "This skepticism about natural causation arose as part of the rejection of the Aristotelian understanding of causation, and finds its logical terminus in Hume's contention that causes and effects are really just events that we observe to be constantly conjoined."

According to my exam paper: "Please discuss."

Signed,

According To How To Write A Business Letter

Dear Future Vice President,

Please discuss? Well, duh. Sounds to me like the first documented historical case of "it's all George Bush's fault." And don't you hate it when skeptics find their logical terminus?

Dear Abby Redux,

I'm the Senate Majority Leader of a fairly popular North American country, and I'm afraid I may lose my bid for re-election. I'm a career politician, and don't know what I would do if I had to get a real job. What do you advise?

Signed,

Hairy Screed

Dear Fossil,

Shut up. "Career" and "politician" should never be used in the same sentence. However, the way you guys have been handling things lately, "politician" and "sentence" are a perfect fit.

Dear Abby Redux,

Loved your column last week. I'm a religious leader who's thinking of starting an advice column of my own, and calling it "Rabbi Redux." Your thoughts?

Signed,

Father Colin del Taco Mgobo Itzhak O'Casey Berkowitz

Dear Hillary's Campaign Manager,
That's the stupidest for an advice column I ever heard.

Dear Abby Redux,

I write a humor column, and recently a lady took me to task for referring to brown pelicans and Helen Thomas as mammals. The lady took the time to point out that pelicans are not mammals. Should I stop writing?

Signed,
Clueless Joe Jackson

Dear Clueless,

That's okay. It's true that pelicans are not mammals. But neither is Helen Thomas.

Dear Abby Redux,

I just took an email test that ended with "think of a color and a tool." Apparently, 98% of people will think of "red hammer." I immediately thought of "white can-opener." I don't even want to consider the therapeutic repercussions.

Signed,
Marginal

Dear Marginal,

You need to butch up. I got two words for you: NAS CAR.

Dear Abby Redux,

Why did the non-causal Aristotelian neorationalist cross the road?

Signed,

Anomimus

Dear Anomimus,

Because he is atavistically self-empowered at a fundoscopic level by an archetypal patristic oneness. To be fair, I just made that up. But, to be equally fair, when you learn how to spell "anonymous," sue me.

Dear Abby Redux,

Your earlier comment about "atavistic self-empowerment at a fundoscopic level" almost sounded dirty!

Signed,

Tee Hee

Dear Future Fox News Host,

Whaddya mean, "almost?"

Dear Abby Redux,

According to a diet expert, I should "eat breakfast like a King, lunch like a Prince, and dinner like a Pauper." I'm confused. What do I do?

Signed,

Rarely Happy

Dear Rarely Happy,

In the morning, invade a country. At noon, release an album called "Purple Rain." And in the evening, vote for a Democrat. Okay, obviously, I'm kidding. Don't vote for a Democrat.

Dear Abby Redux,

In important respects, Damasio's thesis is more a realization than a refutation of the Cartesian program. If I reject neoPlatonics, will I be too big to fail?

Signed,

Gender-Confused Dual Major Coed Who Regularly Wears "Ayn Rand For Commissar" Buttons

Dear Please Shut Up,

Shut up.

Dear Abby Redux,

I just read someone's earlier comment about the possible non-existence of Aristotelian causality. That is UNREAL!

Signed,

No College Classes Before Noon

Dear Future BP CEO,

Your comment is actually funnier than you might have meant.

Dear Abby Redux,

Since Descartes insisted that a mind-body amalgam is a real entity, as opposed to purely passive matter, I see no reason to continue to view him as a dualist.

Signed,

You Wish You Were Dating Me

Dear Yawn-Master,

Let me go out a limb here. In the dictionary, under "fascinating dinner companion," I'm guessing you're listed as an antonym.

Dear Abby Redux,

With Aristotle's laws of motion overthrown, I am lately under the impression that Newton's mechanistic cosmology may have eliminated the need for a deity. Personally, I couldn't care less, but I prosit the presuppostion in hopefully that it may provoke me with extraneous credit on my exam.

Signed,

Red-Shirt Freshman

Dear Red,

Give it a rest, Thesaurus-Boy.

Dear Abby Redux,

I'm the President of a fairly popular North American country, and everything is going wrong. I expected to glide through this on my rhetoric, my chin, and my team of political assassins. Am I getting bad advice?

Signed,

A Profile To Die For

Dear Community Playground Organizer,

Shut up.

Dear Abby Redux,

I'm a collige student who, in order to avoid jail, was forced to take a filosofy class. As part of this week's assignment, several of my classmates and I were instructed to rite you with questions about causality. Is this gonna be on the test?

Signed,

Rhakard Abs

Dear Rhakard Abs,

Good luck in prison.

The Deification of Forest A. Phelps

(Hey. If you can't have faith, have lunch!)

It wasn't your run-of-the-mill classified ad.

"Hi. This is Forest A. Phelps. Last week, I started my own religion and made myself a Reverend. And if you got twenty bucks, I can make *you* a Reverend, too!"

A simple man, a simple idea. What does a person need, anyway, he had often wondered, to parade around calling oneself a "Reverend?" Based on what Forest saw on TV, apparently all you needed was a bad suit and a good deal of gall. True, you might have to do that weird swept-back hair thing; possibly slip on some white patent leather loafers. But a big bucket of gall will get you through that embarrassment. That, and some mousse.

And it was simple enough for Forest to pull it off. He set aside an evening, browsed through the menu of available world religions, cherry-picked the parts he liked and deep-sixed the rest. Then he drew up some ads, bought some mousse, filed some IRS papers, and boom! Forest was a Reverend. And tax-exempt to boot!

Welcome to the Church of Toothless Theology!

As often happens, seemingly unrelated events led Forest to his new career as a local deity. First, the economy was still sulking and people were being laid off in droves. The government was busily implementing an odd strategy of strangling businesses, as if the way to generate more gardens was to kill all the gardeners. People needed hope, and Forest figured he could fake that as well as anybody.

Next, Presidentrix Michelle Obama somehow wandered in front of a TV camera. Before the crew could cut the feed, she started telling everybody to calm down, since there were still thousands of miles of Gulf shoreline that had not been damaged, which might've been cool if there actually *were* thousands of miles of Gulf shoreline, instead of the 1,600-odd miles that, in fact, exist. (Apparently, the Congressional Budget Office drew up her map.)

To clarify any confusion, Joe Biden issued a confusing statement, claiming the White House had saved or created millions of miles of shoreline. (Nor did it sit well when Biden quipped, off-camera, referring to the Gulf of Mexico as "The Dead Sea.") President Profile reminded everybody of his promise not to raise taxes on anyone who lived near an imaginary beach. He renewed his promise to "not rest" until he had saved the Gulf Coast from George Bush, and then flew away to enjoy another vacation. (According to some reports, he didn't take Air Force One; he just flew away.)

Forest watched the news play out and thought, "Not only are people believing these clowns can perform miracles: these clowns are starting to believe it *themselves*. I can fake *that*, too." Given that nobody in the media even blinked in the face of all that extra-natural behavior, Forest couldn't imagine anybody minding if one more messiah hoisted a shop shingle.

And lastly, Forest watched while the NAACP held a press conference and denounced the entire Tea Party movement as a bunch of racists. Suddenly, the Reverend Al Sharpton materialized, followed closely by his hair and by the Reverend Jesse Jackson, who was dressed in a nice, three-piece paternity suit.

Reverend Sharpton, having misunderstood the opening arguments, agreed that the Tea Party was indeed full of racers, and then he indignantly accused New York State of having a city named White Plains. On a roll, Sharpton then chided the city of Pensacola for having white sand beaches, inferring that Pensacola was a veritable hotbed for racers and other spigots. Wrapping up, the Reverend called for a boycott of Arizona, including a demand that the Yankees boycott the upcoming Super Bowl races in Arizona's capital city, Flagpole. Someone pointed out that Sharpton's closing remarks, though hilarious, were not relevant, but Sharpton again misunderstood, arguing that he was, too, a Relevant, and so was his good friend, the Relevant Jesse Johnson.

And with that, Forest had seen all he needed to see. If self-appointed religious leaders, self-righteous politicians, and self-serving citizens were going to act like nothing more than apes in trousers, Forest reckoned he might as well make a buck. He drew up a plan for a shallow, hollow, feel-good religion, mixing anxiety and anesthesia, blending creative marketing with Marx's "opiate for the masses." For a few dollars, he printed up several boxes of direct mail flyers, featuring the name of his new church, its logo (a thumbs-up sign reflected in a mirror) and emboldened with the catchy phrase, "Guilt No More!"

The flyer offered a menu of online classes, a price list, and an extremely comprehensive clutch of legal disclaimers. The curriculum, like the religion itself, was designed to be virtually painless and totally free of any serious commitment (or results). Correspondence courses were offered in various disciplines, including this sampler:

- Justifiable Intolerance: The "Holier Than Thou" Myth
- Creative Accounting I: The Cash Bar Bar-Mitzvah
- Personal Wealth Creation Versus Personal Wealth Evolution
- Witnessing And Eye-Witnessing: How To Work A Jury
- What's So Bad About Bad Words? (The George Carlin Canon)
- Fantasy Writing Challenge: "The Barnacles Of Narnia" (Sponsor: BP)
- Managing Expectations: A Televangelist's Guide To Faith Healing And Litigation
- Creative Accounting II: The Church "Building Fund"
- The "Three Strikes" Rule: How To Get A Mulligan In The Confessional

- Extra-Marital Sex: The New "Weekday" Exemption
- Creative Accounting III: IRS Audits And The "pecunia ex nihilo" Defense
- Deacon Blues: The Search For The Lost Tribe Of Steely Dan
- Off-Shore Banking: A New Take On "Church Planting"
- *Torah! Torah! Torah!*: Jewish Interpretations Of Shinto Shamanism
- The Jawbone Of An Ass: A History Of Religious Indignation In Political Speeches
- Creative Accounting IV: Making The Case For An Emergency Backup Vatican
- The Collected Humor Of Cotton Mather (9:00am to 9:03am)
- Moses And The Ten Suggestions

Prohibitive costs kept the new Reverend from building an actual church facility, but Forest did rent one of those white, changeable-letter roadside signs, and a boxful of black block letters, so he could rotate cute little blurbs at the curb in front of his apartment. During his debut week, he posted the following ill-fated schedule announcement:

SUNDAY MORNING MESSAGE: JESUS WALKED ON THE WATER

SUNDAY EVENING MESSAGE: WHERE IS JESUS?

Forest spent hours in front of the TV, reviewing reruns of several Reverends. From Jimmy Swaggart and Jim Bakker, he learned how to stomp his feet and cry on demand. From Jeremiah Wright, he learned how to dress in comfortable clothes and curse. From Pat Robertson, he learned how to make psychotic remarks. From watching Tammy Faye Bakker, he learned how to change the channel.

But it was from Reverend Jim Jones that Forest learned the importance of food for a fledgling religion. And that made all the difference.

It was Forest's most clever marketing decision: the way he co-packaged cosmic comfort and comfort food to lure a public hungry for both. Faith required trust over time, but a sandwich could be got to right now. And lo, a fast-food franchise was born which, like the new religion itself, offered something for everybody.

Drive-Thru Speaker Voice: Welcome to Self-Actualization Burger! Can I help you help yourself?

Customer: Any specials today?

Voice: You can get two rationalizations for the price of one!

Customer: Nah. I've still got rationalizations left over from last week.

Voice: Well, with every Sheik Shake, we'll throw in an order of French Friars!

Customer: Do you have any waffles that look like one of the Saints?

Voice: Not as such. But you can get a 218-ounce Holy Rolla Cola in a to-go cup that smells like the New Orleans Saints.

Customer: Yeah, that'll do.

Voice: Or you can get a bottle of preservative-free "Saints Preserve Us" holy water.

Customer: Nope. Don't trust your holy water.

Voice: Why not?

Customer: The bottle has an expiration date.

Voice: Point taken.

Customer: And besides, did you realize that "Forest A. Phelps" is an anagram for "False Prophets?"

Voice: That's just uncalled for, sir.

Customer: So, do you guys have Happy Meals, like at McDenials?

Voice: Sir, ALL our meals are Happy Meals!

Customer: How about Esau-sage biscuits, like they have over at Burqa King?

Voice: Sorry, sir. We stop serving breakfast after the Lenten Ramadan mantra chant to Vishnu at Matins.

Customer: Sheesh. Not much of a church, is it.

Voice: Well, we do have a changeable-letter roadside sign, now don't we, Mr. Smarty?

Customer: Big whoop. So does the back-hoe rental place.

Voice: Well, yeah, but our ...

Customer: Forget it. Gimme four Relative Truth-Burgers, two Iced Teleologies and a Forbidden Apple pie.

Voice: Would you like lies with that?

Abby Redux III

(More rants from our grumpy advice columnist)

Dear Abby Redux,

A store in our local paper is advertising "50% off or half price, whichever is less." As a budget-conscious homemaker, I'm conflicted. When should I make my move?

Signed,

Alert Shopper

Dear Alert Shopper,

You should definitely hold out for half price. Afterwards, to celebrate your victory over The System, grab a beverage and spend ninety minutes watching "60 Minutes."

Dear Abby Redux,

I'm very concerned about the long-term effects of the BP oil spill on our seafood. Am I being overly cautious?

Signed,

Al B. Chronic

Dear Al,

Shut up. Those nice folks at BP are just cutting out the middleman. Remember: for years now, we've been buying cans of tuna fish packed in oil. Maybe, if we're lucky, BP will take the next logical step and come up with a way to spill mayonnaise and chopped celery.

Dear Abby Redux,

I just heard that Florida's Governor is thinking about switching parties again. Again! What is it with all these politicians changing parties? Which party is he switching to now?

Signed,
Beachcomber Babs

Dear Babs,

Tupperware.

Dear Abby Redux,

A clothing store at the mall is advertising "wonderful bargains for men with 16 or 17 necks." I don't understand.

Signed,
Ima Littledim

Dear Yes You Are,

It's a simple question, dearie. Does your husband have 32 arms, or 34? Just shop for the shirt with the right number of necks, and hope the store's got a deal going on gloves. By the way, have you heard about the 50% off sale?

Dear Abby Redux,

Next month, I'm planning to attend my 35th high school reunion. Talk about your target-rich environment! Any suggestions on what I should wear?

Signed,

Single Again

Dear Sepia Centerfold,

Let's face some facts, Toots. No need to dust off the open-toed shoes for this one. Thirty-five years *since* high school? All the women's hair will be dyed, and all the men's hair will *have* died. Unsaddle the steed of your stellar standards; you're not gonna rope in "Mr. Right" this night. Orville or Wilbur Wright, maybe. You'll be lucky to snag a dance with "Mr. Still Upright." Wear something comfortable. Avoid the punch.

Dear Abby Redux,

I'm one of them guys whats always lookin to better hisself. Yesterday I seen a Help Wanted ad like this here - "Tired of working for only $9.75 an hour? Profit sharing, flexible hours. Starting pay: $7-$9 per hour." Huzzah! My ship has drove in!

Signed,

Burl

Dear Burl,

You know, somewhere in your town sits one seriously depressed math teacher. But buck up, Burl, and seize the moment. Settle for nothing less, my boy. With crack analytical skills like yours, you'll claw your way to the nearest nadir in no time. And no, Burl, "nadir" does not mean "more nade."

Dear Abby Redux,

For his 35th birthday, we bought a go-cart for our son, Sheldon, who still lives with us. The go-cart instructions include a rather sobering warning that states, "Object Moves When In Use." Do you think giving our child such a hazardous play-pretty would be irresponsible?

Signed,
Mrs. Sheldon Alabaster Pinckney IV

Dear Mrs. Sheldon-Person,

If I were you, I wouldn't worry about the go-kart's "object will move" warning; instead, slap a sign on young Sheldon that says "Object will move out and get a job already."

Dear Abby Redux,

I did a lot of drugs in the 60s, and I think it's catching up with me. The other night on the news, I could've sworn I heard President Obama telling NASA to knock it off with all that "spaceship" stuff and focus their high-tech talents on a new mission: morale-boosting pep rallies for Muslim nations. Pardon me? NASA?

Signed,
Allen Haylitt

Dear Allen,

Shut up. What's NASA done for us? Tang. It's high time we got more for our money than a roomful of crew cuts, short-sleeved white shirts and pocket-protectors. I mean, it's not like NASA went to the *moon* or anything. Next, I suppose, the White House will task the Postmaster General with reviewing Broadway plays, and the National Endowment for the Arts will be managing suburban HVAC repair. Obviously.

Dear Abby Redux,

This week, I saw a Facebook ad suggesting that people "Explore Gay Hawaii." Since then, I keep getting these mental images of Fred Flintstone in a hula skirt.

Signed,
Name Withheld

Dear Congressman,

Whatever you're currently spending on therapy, bump up the budget.

Dear Abby Redux,

Somehow, I got pregnant. I think it happened over the internet. Should I go to a male or a female gynecologist?

Signed,
Anita Epidural

Dear Probably Walks Around Humming Cartoon Themes,

Well, that depends. Do you want to have a boy or a girl?

Dear Abby Redux,

This week, the White House announced a 16-member commission to study exports. I think that says it all. The current administration has obviously saved us from ourselves, the worst is over, and it truly is the Summer of Recovery in America.

Signed,

Hope N. Change

Dear Prius Owner,

Exports, in this economy? Are you kidding me? *What* exports? We don't even export illegal aliens. On the other hand, this action is sure to save or create 16 Export Commission jobs. Or one job for a guy I know who has 16 necks.

Dear Abby Redux,

Every single day, it seems like some dumb store prints some dumb ad, hoping we're dumb enough to fall for it. One store is advertising a "Three-Day Sale! Friday Only." Another is yelling "Stock up now and save! Limit 1." The corner gas station says they're "open 7 days a week, and weekends." And our local grocery is hawking "Georgia

Peaches. California grown." How dumb do these people think we are?

Signed,

Guy That Lives Alone

Dear Closet Full of 'Members Only' Jackets,

Send me only $9.95 and I'll tell you how dumb you are. Act now and I'll throw in some fresh peaches from San Diego, Georgia.

Thursday, As I Evolved

(If we're voting, here's mine: ALL surgery is invasive.)

Last week, I had a little run-in with some pain. Which is kind of like saying that, in the 1940s, Europe had a little run-in with Hitler.

One thing you young guys out there should know. As you grow older, there are going to be some great events coming your way. People to hold and to hold on to. Memories to cherish, mental photographs to capture, treasure and recall.

None of those wonderful, cherished moments will ever, ever have anything to do with your butt.

Monday, I seemed to be fine. Tuesday, I began to notice some political correctness. True, Wednesday morning's book study at a local coffee shop did leave me feeling a bit insulted by the shop's rather Spartan decisions regarding chair selection, but I soldiered on and got back home.

And then, by Wednesday evening, the discussion was over. BP had attacked my Gulf.

By Thursday morning, I had morphed into a hideous thing, with virtually no shot at becoming the next poster boy for Posture Pals. When I walked or otherwise moved, it hurt my HAIR. The slightest of activities was unwelcome, including cell mitosis. I was galumphing around my house like a "Shrek" computer animation glitch.

Neville Chamberlain rang up and suggested I wait a while, and maybe Hitler would calm down and BP would just go away. I made an admittedly unfair comparison between Neville's face and a ferret's gulf, and Neville rang off. Then I headed out for the doctor's.

I'd never really thought about it before, but as it turns out, you *can* actually drive a car without ever once touching the car seat. (Traffic ticket management tip: opt for less-travelled roads)

At the doctor's, it was all professionalism.

"Sweetie, we're swamped - can you come back in an hour?"

"Have you ever met Neville Chamberlain?"

"Pardon?"

An hour later, I drove back in.

"Ah, Mr. Shrek. The doctor will see you now, honey."

"Ahl em blesh. Fnee tlum."

"Pardon?"

I proceeded to the "the doctor will have his way with you now" room and was told to "prep," which is doctor-office-speak for "Remove all the clothes your parents told you never to remove in public, put on this cheesy Toga outfit, and lie down on top of that roll of butcher paper, on that table we just pulled out of the upright freezer in the garage." So I prepped, fell in the general direction of the examining table, and faced the wall. And a few minutes later, I heard the doctor utter one of those highly technical medical diagnoses you just never want to hear when you're "prepped" and facing a wall.

"Wow."

I was immediately referred to a surgeon some 10 miles away, which meant I had to cope with, and survive, another drive. So I strapped into my impromptu zero-Gee modified seatbelt harness, bit down on a large stick, and triple-clutched my way across town.

Ultimately, everything worked out. I think. Maybe it didn't, and I'm dead. It's late June in South Carolina, so it's hard to tell. So before I proceed, let me go ahead and share some handy advice with you. Someday, somewhere, you're bound to find yourself in an unexpected conversational situation. A comment will catch you by surprise. I mean, some things, you just never really expected (or wanted) to hear. So here are some possible replies to awkward chat.

(Paid Professional)
"Please undress, lie down, and face the wall."

(Your Options)

- Aw, honey. I didn't get *you* anything.
- Don't I get a phone call?
- Hey! Are you *sure* this is the Real Estate seminar?

(Paid Professional)
"Wow."

(Your Options)

- That's what they all say.
- Now don't go getting technical on me.
- That's kind of you, but I still think we should see other people.

(Paid Professional)
"Does this hurt?"

(Your Options)

- I've had worse.
- Aw, you palpate like my sister.
- Please speak up. I'm screaming.

(Paid Professional)
"Okay, now we're going to tape together your buttocks."

(Your Options)

- No, you are *NOT*.
- Well now, *there's* something you don't hear every day.
- Ever done time, Doc?
- Really? You mean I'm finally going on "Dancing With The Stars?"

But my story ends well. The kind surgeon performed a few "Full Monty" outtakes, and ... boom ... the pain went away. Just ... went away. I could even drive home without duct-taping myself to the sun visor.

The human body. What a wonderful, complex, largely self-regulating machine we have; this human body; this gift; this miraculous mechanism that some interesting people still think was created entirely at random, one mutation at a time, eh?

But I had the rest of Thursday afternoon to kill anyway, so I went ahead and evolved. That car-seat levitation thing could come in handy, especially at concerts, so I willed that into permanency. Added a short third arm, too, at the base of my back, just as a backup prop-up. I evolved myself free of ear-lobe hair (never did understand where evolution was headed with *that* one). And because I've had surgery, I made another minor comfort adjustment. I still take in food through my mouth, but now I discharge it from my armpit.

Hah. Wait till the "fossil record" gets a load of *me*.

But it's all good. Between me and my third arm, we're a shoe-in for the next Posture Pals.

Abby Redux IV

(Dealing with the public begins to wear on our favorite irritated columnist)

EDITORIAL SIDEBAR: Abby's physician, concerned about her steadily increasing blood pressure, has requested that we, for a time, censor your queries to filter out political topics. As we share a concern for Abby's well-being, we shook the physician's hand and agreed; furthermore, we were, quite frankly, lying between our teeth. Suck it up, Abby.

Dear Abby Redux,

Did you see this headline in the paper? "South Carolina man gets 7 years for sex crime."

Signed,

Confused In Carolina

Dear Confused,

I understand why you're confused. That's just nuts. No way it can take him seven years.

Dear Abby Redux,

Someone named Rankhaj keeps sending me emails, offering me a "fulfillingly software" job, at "a waging of your desires," in a South Carolina town called Creyer (pronounced "Cur"). I'm open to relocating, but I'm conflicted. I wonder if Rankhaj is cute? For that matter, do you think Rankhaj is male or female? Do you think the job will offer good benefits and insurance?

Signed,

Androgynous In Alabama

Dear Androgynous,

Hard to say. For some reason that's never been explained, software recruiters always sound like they come from a country that has elephants. Either way, I recommend you take the plunge. Life is too short (probably, so is Rankhaj). So go get 'em! You should know, though, that I've been to Cur, South Carolina. You might very well get a nice benefits package, but in Cur, they don't have much need for dental insurance.

Dear Abby Redux,

Did you see this newspaper headline? "South Carolina man gets 7 years for sex crime."

Signed,

Challenged In Charlotte

Dear Challenged,

Yeah, I saw it. Seven years. Now that's what I call lethargy. Imagine getting stuck behind that guy at the grocery check-out.

EDITORIAL ASIDE: [Hey, Fred! Watch this!]

Dear Abby Redux,

What's wrong? I see that you're taking intravenous medication this week. I hope everything works out okay!

Signed,

At Large In Atlanta

Dear At Large,

Shut up. That's not what Abby Redux "IV" means, for Pete's sake. It doesn't mean "IV tube." It means "four." Honestly, I sometimes wonder how you people manage to walk and chew tobacco at the same time.

Dear Abby Redux,

What's all this hullabaloo about "sanctuary cities?" Look, if some town wants to have a church, that ought to be none of our dadburn business.

Signed,

Bothered In Butte

Dear Bothered,

What a clever observation! Just wondering. How do you pronounce "Butte?"

Dear Abby Redux,

Did you see this headline? "South Carolina man gets 7 years for sex crime."

Signed,

Chaste In Charleston

Dear Chaste,

Yes, I did. You gotta admire the man's dedication. Speaking personally, after about six months, I'd just give up and find some other crime to commit.

Dear Abby Redux,

Did you see this headline? "South Carolina woman finds cheeseburger in gas tank."

Signed,

Alert In Asheville

Dear Alert,

What is it with South Carolina? And what was this woman doing in her gas tank?

EDITORIAL SIDEBAR: Here comes another one. I know: we promised. We can't help ourselves.

Dear Abby Redux,

Did you see this story? Congressman Rangel, brought before the Ethics Committee for using his "public servant" position to cut deals, has cut a deal with the Ethics Committee.

For any single one of these "ethics violations," you or I would be put in "subsidized federal housing." I thought that overly-dentate Pelosi mammal told us she was gonna "drain the swamp?"

Signed,

Disgusted In Des Moines

Dear Disgusted,

Shut up. In case you hadn't heard, justice has prevailed. For his dozen-plus ethics violations, the Congress is gonna make Rangel stand in front of the whole room. The whole room!

EDITORIAL ASIDE: [Nice!]

EDITORIAL ASIDE: [Thanks, Fred!]

Dear Abby Redux,

I'm really looking forward to the next Presidential Library. Long ago, there was the pure power of President Jefferson: "We hold these truths to be self-evident." Then came the immortal prose of President Lincoln: "Four score and seven years ago." Now, there's President Profile: "Hey! We got Orlando in the house."

Signed,

"Eft" Gingrich

Dear Other-Useless-Spokesman,

At least he can pronounce "nuclear." And spell "potato." As Joe Biden would say, "I got three words for you. Shut up."

Dear Abby Redux,

Did you hear this story? During today's taping of President Profile's guest appearance on "The View," several irrelevant citizens were tragically killed when an expanding-out-of-all-control Adoration Bomb violently interacted with the President's inherent ego cloud.

Signed,

Former First Lady

Dear 2012 Presidential Hopeful,

This week's topic was supposed to be news headlines. How did these political comments sneak in here?

EDITORIAL SIDEBAR: Oops.

Dear Abby Redux,

Did you see this headline? "South Carolina cops look for ties in missing woman cases."

Signed,

Rattled In Raleigh

Dear Rattled,

Let me guess. The ties could not be reached for comment.

Dear Abby Redux,

Did you see this headline? "South Carolina man says car hit him." The victim said the driver of a blue "box style" Oldsmobile swerved and hit him with the passenger side bumper. The victim told officers he thought the suspect hit him on purpose and he, the victim, wanted to "press full charges" against the suspect, who the victim said was about 50 years old and, the victim had reason to believe, might be employed at a local packing plant.

Signed,

Sordid In Salinas

Dear Sordid,

The victim "had reason to believe" where the suspect worked? I'm gonna go out a limb here. Behind this story, there's a Victim X, a Suspect Y, and a Wife Z, aka Mrs. Y, whose youngest child looks a whole lot like X. There may even be a future Packing Plant employee named X Junior, or however they spell "X" down there in Cur.

Dear Abby Redux,

Did you see this headline in the paper? "South Carolina man gets 7 years for sex crime."

Signed,

Tepid In Tempe

Dear Tepid,

Yes, I did. And we thought you Southerners just *talked* slowly.

Dear Abby Redux,

Did you see this headline? "South Carolina man says car hit him."

Signed,

Packed In Oil In Pendleton

Dear Packed,

I did see that. Do you suppose they called in the sketch artist? Imagine *that* conversation:

"Yeah, officer. About 50, I reckon. Ugly, overly-dentate feller. Smelled like a packing plant."

"Smelled like a *what*?"

Dear Abby Redux,

What exactly do they do in a "packing plant?"

Signed,

Unnamed Illegant Immigral, Working At The Lazy Dubya Potatoe Ranch

Dear Undocumented Voter,

I'm afraid to ask. And I wonder, too, about the police report's reference to "a" packing plant. How many packing plants do you suppose they've got in this burg?

By the way: "illegant immigral?" You're gonna fit right in, here in America.

Dear Abby Redux,

Over a period of seven years, my boss at the packing plant hypnotized me on a magic couch and then committed various ethics violations involving overly-dentate mammals wearing ties. Now I'm being unfairly accused of using a cheeseburger-powered Prius to keep independent voters from Tea Party rallies!

Signed,

Rankhaj Rangel

Oy. Dear Editorial Department,

I need a vacation. What's wrong with these people? I'll say it again: No Politics This Week!

EDITORIAL SIDEBAR: We're particularly fond of that last one. Oh! Remember the "IV Tube" letter? We wrote that one, too.

Is this fun, or what?

This Could Take a While

(Eternity. It just won't end. I think that's the point.)

Forever. Considering what we've managed to do to ourselves in just a few thousand years, humans may need a while to adjust to such a concept. We're gonna need a little time for forever.

"So this is eternity? Man. Where's the remote, dog? This is taking *forever*."

Yeah. Forever could take a while.

"Forever" is a term we humans throw around all the time, without much thought or respect.

- "This is maddening! I've been on hold forever!"
- "I'll love you forever."
- "Whoa. I haven't heard *that* song in forever!"
- "lol ur not kidding lol 2days meetings taking 4ever rotf"
- "Nope. No more software upgrades. Period. This new version will last forever!" (always said, somehow, with a straight face)

I'm guilty, too. I remember once describing a singer as holding a note "forever." The first time I ever heard Rachelle Ferrell, she was the opener for Al Jarreau in Atlanta's Chastain Park. During one song, she grabbed a note, planted her feet, and then time stood still. Gape-jawed, I watched her work that note for about three weeks, then I took off to do a little shopping, then drove to Charleston, ate some shrimp, bought a house, had it re-roofed, drove back to Atlanta – and she was Still. Wearing. That. Note. Out.

I mean, the lady has *PIPES*. Later in her set, while having her way with a lazy tune in g-minor, she found so many steps between F# and G that an Andean tribe planted maize.

Humans don't yet have a respect for forever. We're in much too much of a hurry. We want now, and we want now *now*. For the most part, the people I run into are extremely unprepared for *anything* that never ends. We've barely enough patience for things that *end*, like childhood, and gratitude, and Paris Hilton's career. We have Cliff Notes. Precooked food. Uncooked food (sushi). Overnight shipping. Group weddings. Quickie Divorce. Ears Pierced While You Wait. Instant coffee. Loan approvals over the phone. Drive-thru churches. Automatic weapons.

We've even managed to create devices that let us skip commercials. Commercials! We can't stand to sit still for *sixty seconds*.

Fortunately, forever promises to be a great deal more than just an endless buffet of Life As We Now Know

It. Because I'll be honest: if eternity means Twentieth-Century-Culture-Without-End, I don't want that channel.

Douglas Adams, a wonderful writer, once wrote a series of science fiction stories that involved a hitchhiker, a galaxy, at least one two-headed guy, several robots and, of course, billions and billions of thick, clueless, government bureaucrats. One of Mr. Adams' characters was an immortal who had finally, over time, just simply gotten sick of the whole "immortality" idea. According to this jaded alien, the worst thing about living forever was Sunday afternoons. And I can see her or his or its point, because Sunday afternoons, even here on temporal Earth, can seem to go on for ... well ... forever, especially during bowling season.

But Eternity? That's fringe. Eternity deals in numbers that are simply impossible to grasp, unless you're up for re-election in Congress, or are working for the current administration's Treasury Department.

We're not ready, in our current condition, for forever. We might end up like Mr. Adams' alien, who decided to burn a few billion millennia by traveling the entire universe, introducing her/him/itself to every single living being, in alphabetical order. Nice theory, I suppose, but in practice it just ended up making the alien even *more* depressed, what with mortals running around rudely dying all over the place. And worse yet, rudely not dying in alphabetical order.

Here's a thought: living forever will let us ride along, till the end of time, and try to imagine what nonsense marketing departments will come up with next.

The possibilities are endless. Recently I heard that some group was marketing a mouthwash called "Smart-Mouth." See what I mean? Someone has named an oral hygiene product after a playground insult.

Hey, don't stare at *me*. I'm just telling you what I *heard*.

Personally, though, I probably need a product more along the lines of "Smart-Mouth-B-Gone."

Smart-Mouth-B-Gone! Now in Alpine Mint! Try Smart-Mouth-B-Gone today! Now available in Small, Medium, Large, X-Large, Huge Issues, Do-You-Kiss-Your-Mother-With-That-Mouth, and Joe Biden!

Living forever will also let us observe just how far the human race will ultimately go with these Reality TV shows. Way back when, in my childhood, we had "Candid Camera." Nowadays, I understand we have an updated version called "Punk'd," and I'm grateful for it, because without "Punk'd" I might never have known that we had replaced the letter e with an apostroph'.

I gu'ss it's tru': you'r' n'v'r too old to l'arn.

And now Iraqi TV has apparently raised the bar. They have a new reality show where a bomb is planted in the car of local celebrities, and the celebrities are then accused of being terrorists. Then, I guess, there's a commercial break (*"The all-new instant lettuce! Now in brown or brown!"*) and after the break we all gather round to watch as hilarity ensues.

Here's another example of "ever" abuse. Although I think I know where the sports network was trying to go with the concept, ESPN University's new ad campaign, *NEVER GRADUATE*, may be sending some mixed signals.

C'mon. Never graduate? *Ever?* I mean, eventually, you're gonna run out of beer.

Way back when, lots of things were different. Better than now? Yeah, some of it. We might go entire months at a time without a single disfiguring accident on "Candid Camera." There were definitely less news stories featuring the phrases "disgruntled employee" and "spray of bullets." Back then, Christmas was a nationally-accepted season of shared happiness and joy and peace, rather than the foul, unenlightened, non-inclusive, social-fabric-destroying, offensive ritual that it's accused of being today. And irony was a literary device, not a political strategy.

But Eternity has potential. Being around for all of time could have its advantages, too. Let's ponder a few:

- You can eat whatever you want. No worries - you're dead! Ever eat a whole stick of butter?
- After you eat, there'll be no need to wait a half-hour before you can go swimming.
- No more calorie warnings, carb counts, trans-fat neuroses, egg-part parsing, beef restrictions, pork issues (actually, we're still researching the pork thing).
- You can mess up and drop food on the floor. No "count to three" rule anymore. Go ahead. Leave it

on the floor. Leave it for twenty, forty, fifty trillion years. Pick it up and eat it. No worries. You're dead!

- If the day should ever come, we'll be there to watch when Amazon.com announces its first profit.
- Eventually, based on current immigration patterns, Mexico will be empty. Maybe somebody will convert the country into a great big hot tub, or a megamall.
- We'll get to see how long George Bush continues to get blamed for stuff. My guess is that one day, there will be no more stuff, and George Bush will be blamed for the fact that there is no more stuff.
- Sooner or later, Joe Biden will say something accurate. I mean ... surely. Eventually. Surely. Won't he?

I suppose that in any discussion about life, death and forever, we ought to touch on ghosts. Unfortunately, I have even less useful knowledge about dead ghosts than I have about live women, and that should give you a huge clue as to how short this "ghost" section's gonna be.

Recently, some lady started telling me a story about a Lesbian ghost that was haunting her. Because I wasn't fast enough to get off the bus, she continued her story. I honestly couldn't follow much of the plot, what with my constant lunges for the "stop" cord. But it seems that, in addition to all your standard ghost-type internal conflicts and spook-specific career challenges, this Lesbian ghost kept trying to change the diapers of the haunted woman's child. I bet you don't see a lot of *that* in the Baghdad suburbs.

I guess I need to rethink the whole role of ghosts as passengers on my Forever Ferry. If a dead person can have a sexual orientation so unfulfilled that they run around haunting talkative mothers on public transportation, and performing toilet tasks for their toddlers, maybe I just won't die.

A Forever, not free from phobias and class warfare? An Eternity, with a bureaucracy? Good grief. Imagine how complicated the 2,000,000,000,000,010 Census will be!

Should be a good gig for the lawyers, though. Death's never stopped *them*:

"If you've been the victim of a wrongful death, call Legal Buddies now! Even though you're dead, you have rights! Don't wait. Call now and ask about our "post-mortem" discount. But call now, because this offer won't last forev..."

Of course, other than one blurry "homecoming" weekend in college, I have no experience with being dead. So I don't know how you tell if you're really dead or not. Maybe it'll be quite obvious. Or maybe being dead works like being insane: as long as you're wondering if you are, you probably aren't.

To wrap things up, I guess we'd better point out some of the disadvantages to being around forever. Witness:

- Billions and billions of Fleetwood Mac reunions
- Trees may die out. Where will we get our calendars?

- You'll get no sympathy whatsoever for remarks like, "Man, this download is taking *forever!*"
- The inevitable debut episode of "Dancing With The Neutrino Super-Novas"
- Endless, endless, endless trips to the grocery to replace batteries for your latest smart phone implant, the Apple iSkull.
- Government Stimulus Plan # 836.3 cubed x 923 to the 1,467th power (I can just hear Joe Biden now: "Trust me - *this* one has the magic.")
- The eternally-looming threat of another "Die Hard" sequel
- I'm guessing that, after a few hundred million trillion years or so, our Sun will go dark. Then they'll have to recalibrate their whole "global warming" argument. And they'll have to blame *somebody*. Five bucks says it won't be the Lesbian ghost.

"Smart-Mouth." Whew. To come up with that one, I'll bet marketing sat through meetings (and cross-channel leveraged evaluations, and weekend getaway break-outs, and transient ergotropic analyses, and double-blind Gannt-slope bell-curved non-integrated focus groups) for, well...

...forever.

Wonder what they'll call th' laxativ'?

Intermission

Clay Pigeons

(To Jessie Julien: For teaching me to look within the words for the pictures)

The last day of the month crawled by. It crawled like the afternoon sun crawled, a sun unseen but for its subtle siblings, an army of fleeting images, forming and fleeing along the tier of windshields in the cars parked in front of Taylor's small store. Bright, far too bright, these beacons winked on and off, glaring at Taylor as he walked here and there in his store, going about his business, going about his attempts to avoid his business, going about his efforts to try and ignore the fact that there was no business.

One of the last remaining constants of Taylor's job was the slow but sure approach, every afternoon, of the blinding reflections sired by the sun in the cars huddled across the no-parking zone. Now and again Taylor would stare at those refracted spotlights for as long as he could stand it, then turn his head, close his eyes and watch the ghosts of those spotty lights play across the insides of his eyelids. Playing, like tiny wounded and confused birds, circling, unsure where to go.

And the children come and go, don't you know.

Suddenly the door swung open. There had once been an electronic bell on the door that would burble and chime its welcome to each new customer, but that chime had burned itself out in the glory days, those days when it would sing out hundreds of times each week, heralding hoards of descending shoppers. Of that bell there now remained only a very subtle electronic buzzing, something that only Taylor could still hear. He had been in this store far too long. Hours of dulling ritual and rote conditioning caused him to lift his head, almost subconsciously, to gaze toward the front door.

Taylor regrouped, re-entering real (real?) life. He inwardly moaned as he focused upon an image – walking up the aisle was an old man, dressed in a barely baggy blue suit ("natty," Taylor thought, wondering if that was the right word), wearing (sporting?) a perfectly tilted pork-pie hat on his white hair. Full beard, thick eyebrows, large-rimmed glasses which magnified bright and alert eyes. Taylor was reminded of a retired life insurance salesman, copious with canned wit and less-than-captivating anecdotes. He was half-right.

The old man stopped just inside the door, looking over the first bank of shelves, silently reinforcing Taylor's initial impression -- here was one more jerk just wasting his time, killing time, marking time. He was half-right.

As the gentleman sidled up the aisle and closed on the counter, Taylor got up and turned off the loud and violent movie he was watching, rotating the switch on the amp over to the tuner selection, filling the building with classical music. He sat back down.

Taylor looked very intently at absolutely nothing, waiting for the old guy to launch into whatever it was that made these browsers feel the need to take totally helpless strangers into their confidence, waiting for whatever it was that caused them to spew forth a fountain of banality.

This time, though, Taylor was dead wrong. The old man began.

"Howya doin, young fellah? I'm waitin fuh th' wife over in the store, there, and waitin here, cause it's much cooler in here, donchaknow, yes, that air condition sure does feel so much bettah, donchaknow?"

Taylor, perpetually the retail host, slipped on a mildly Southernized accent, like a debutante might slide into an appropriate outfit. "Well, you just make yourself right at home, there," he said, watching the old guy sink slowly into the deeps of the little couch lining the left wall.

"You know, that reminds me," the old man puttered, "there was this song that the kids use-ta sing there in the Apistopal Church, donchaknow, actually, it, uh, sorta started out as a, well, a, sorta black-sounding thing, and the chorus went...

'Sit down, children, and close the door
And you'll hear Bible stories like you never heard before.
We come to Sunday School each week from our home,
So sit down, children, and make yourself at home...'"

Taylor slung a glance toward the ceiling, that universal gesture that means, "Oh, Jeez..."

"Well, and then," the dapper little man continued, slipping into second gear, "there was the first verse, about, uh, about Cain hitting Abel on his head and Abel fell down dead, donchaknow, then, well, the second verse came along next, donchaknow, which went on something about Jonah catching a ride on the whale...no, on the trans-Alanic whale, and the one about David, and a Moses one, and it went on and on, donchaknow, but, you work here full-time?"

Taylor blinked. From Moses to full-time retail, huh? From 'Let my people go' to 'Let my people go shopping?' Well, okay. He sighed. "Yessir, I do."

The old man nodded. "My son got in this business, back when it was still a new thing, donchaknow, and, and, well I doan think he did real well at it, but it's, uh, you work here full-time?"

And the children come and go, don't you know.

"Yes, Sir." clarified Taylor. "I still do." Catching Taylor's general drift, the natty dresser moved on.

"Do you go to college, young man?"

"No, Sir, I'm through. I finished."

"When did you finish?"

Taylor looked up at the ceiling and squinted a bit, as though hunting through hazes of obscure time. "Uh, 19...81."

"No, come away!" the old man grinned. "You look to be about 21 years old!"

"Thirty-one," Taylor grinned back.

The old man's head made one quick jerk to the side, almost qualifying as a nervous tic, and looked up. "Make that music turn up, wouldja?"

Without knowing it, the verbose and spark-eyed man had hit a warm spot with that request, stoking the deep-banked fires of Taylor's love for music. "I sure will," Taylor smiled. "I'll be glad to."

This guy's head works like a doggone pinball machine, Taylor thought. It's like, every thirty seconds, he's slap-happy and running, off on some tangent, every bouncing thought as exotic as the vitamin-charged shouting that the announcers at South Florida dog tracks spout over the track microphone before each race, clarions thumping the crowd into rushes of excitement..."AND THEY'RE OFF!!"

The old man's head, still slightly canted to one side, tuned in to the duck prints on the wall behind the couch, and BOOM went the pinball machine inside his head. He rolled on.

"You know, these ducks here remind me of those old clay pigeons, ones the hunters shoot down, donchaknow, ones they call, what they use-ta, they call 'skeet,' you know what skeet is, young man?"

Taylor smiled distantly as he looked at the wizened little man on the couch. Taylor had suddenly remembered times when his dad had taken him out to the open South Carolina fields, father and son armed with loaded shot-guns.

They would stand on a mark, aim and yell "PULL!" Cued by that command, from either of two square silos flanking the "hunters," a mechanical arm would sling a small round disc skyward, a sculpted and suicidal clay plate, which the armed Americans would try to eliminate from the planet.

This helped to build a real man.

The memory clicked into place and then Taylor's mind reeled, skidding back to this very real last day of the month. "Sure, I know what skeet are."

"Clay pigeons," the ancient man continued. "They use-ta be called, ayuh, but they use-ta use real pigeons, donchaknow."

"Tsat right?"

"Yeah, they use-ta use real pigeons, they would cage 'em from the cities, donchaknow, when they started putting up the skyscrapers, they use-ta capture those live pigeons and bring 'em out to the shootin ranges, donchaknow. They even, I believe they even had these trappers, that would, they'd pay these trappers to cage the pigeons, the building owners, they would, since the pigeons would, you know how they would mess up the owner's buildings.

"So they'd pay these trappers, and they'd bring the pigeons down to the shootin ranges. Course, they would clip one of the wings so the pigeons couldn't... they would clip just a bit off one wing, they couldn't clip too much, or the pigeons couldn't fly 'tal, I think, I think if you clip off, say, more than 'bout, say, one-fiff of the wing, they couldn't... but just enough to make, so the pigeons just flew some erratic, donchaknow."

"Tsat right," Taylor mumbled. He'd had another flash of memory during his guest's last outburst.

He recalled other times when his dad would take him out to other fields, where Taylor would see a phalanx of pick-up trucks (meaning a dog trainer, or maybe a police-man), station wagons (meaning a hardware salesman, or maybe a fledgling RealEstateGuy), the occasional Mercedes (doctor, lawyer, or maybe a career RealEstateGuy). Cars and trucks, all parked in a line.

After a little milling about and gratuitous hand-shaking, the group would grab their shotguns and march out into the field. The field was always the same – a cleared circle of bare ground, wrapped around a wooded area which stood in the middle, a great green Christmas bow on a present for someone very special. Stakes had been driven into the ground at regular intervals like numbers on a watch-face, around the circular copse of thick green woods. These stakes served as stations for the "Hunters."

Completely hidden inside the great green Christmas bow (and completely unknown to Taylor his first time out) was a guy with a flat-bed truck. This guy was the commander of a clutch of small cages, each petite cell imprisoning a live pheasant, a beautiful and graceful bird.

Taylor now found himself wondering if those pheasants had had, say, just about one-fifth of their wings clipped.

All the brave woodsmen would eventually take their place at one or another of the stakes, bellying up to the gene pool bar, testosterone-and-tonics, and each round on the house. Before the festivities would commence, the good ole boys would toss around jokes and insults, deer-hunting lies and woman-conquering myths...

"Yeah, man, I sure do love that South Florida. I get me more dates than a 13-month calendar."

"Aw, fool, you couldn't get a date if you was a palm tree!"

"...and then, well I swear foduh law, that blasted deer just walked right into the back of my truck!"

"Shucks, that durn Jimmy, I swear, he'd rather climb a tree an' tell a lie than stay on the ground an' tell the truth."

And the children come and go, don't you know.

At some specified cue which Taylor could never figure out, the guy in the truck inside the great green Christmas bow would open one of the prison cells, releasing one of the doomed (crippled?) pheasants. The pheasant would tear up and out of the great green Christmas bow of death, probably amazed at its instant parole, only to be splatted out of the sky by whichever of the Hunters was closest to its erratic flight path. Sometimes three or four of the Hunters would take a shot, turning the surprised pheasant into attic dust.

Boy, that's some fun. Boy, that's some hunting prowess.

The old man's pinball machine clinked and buzzed, pulling Taylor back, back to this little man, here on the last day of the month.

"Yes sir, real pigeons," Mr. Pinball continued, "with their wings just clipped enough so they'd fly, just erratic some, donchaknow. Me and these other fellahs one time..." (again, Taylor could hear that track announcer..."AND THEY'RE OFF!!") "...went down to...took a private car to...son, do you know what a private car is?"

"You mean on a train, a sleeper car?"

"Yes, a sleeper ca...well, it was really a chartered car, at the back of the train, and you could charter the whole car, for a trip, donchaknow, and me and these fellahs were going down to Florida for a hunting party. These fellahs were some real gamblers, loved to bet on just about anything 'tal, donchaknow, fact is, we..." He paused, as though his throat had suddenly dried, as though he as stepped on a valuable icon. As though he had opened a door better left shut.

"Well, we were going down to shoot at some of those real pigeons. This was back in, I think, in 1937, and I was just about to get marr...back in 1938, I think...before I met my wife, this was the 23rd of July in 1938, I had gone to Europe...you ever been to Europe?"

Taylor set out to say that he had not. "No, I haven't, but everyone in my family ha--"

The old man began firing away again. "And the best thing happened, as I met a young girl, there in Europe, but she just stayed there an' I came on back home to Charleston, so she had...you married, young man?"

The pinball machine was sho' nuff hummin' now.

"No, Sir, I'm not."

The pork-pie hat stood up. "Well, that's another reason you ought to go to Europe!" he said with a wide yellow-toothed grin.

Proud of his humour, he left the couch and walked over to confront Taylor at the counter. He took off his glasses and began to wipe them with a light blue handkerchief from his inside coat pocket.

Natty, natty, natty.

"Met the most wonderful kind of girl, but she stayed there in Europe, donchaknow. Well, came to find out that she had gotten a job in St. Thomas, donchaknow, down in the Virgin Islands there, and I was sittin down to 2:00 dinner at my...do you know what '2:00 dinner' is, young man?"

Taylor had begun to get increasingly captivated by whatever relentless, stream-of-consciousness Demon it was that ejected this furious and relentless barrage of stories from within the old guy's arsenal, and he now found himself completely hooked. This, his mind told him, should be fascinating.

What an idiot.

"2:00 dinner?" Taylor replied. "No, I don't believe I know what that is."

"Well," the pinball arsenal continued, "that's when you sit down to eat at 2:00!"

Taylor's smile, interest, patience, all began to fade as he realized what an idiot he'd been for asking into the mystery of the "2:00 dinner." He decided to drop back and punt. "Well, I've really got a lot of work t--"

"See," the old man interrupted, gripping the counter, tilting his head and leaning back, "everybody use-ta sit down to dinner here at 2:00 here in Charleston, donchaknow, and they, everybody use-ta have servants back then, donchaknow, before World War One, after World War One nobody could afford servants any more, after that, uh..."

The old man paused, his face clouded as if entangled in some mental overload. Taylor's own face screwed up in confusion. "I really don't see the connec--"

"But this young thing had moved to St. Thomas to work, that's down in the Virgin Islands, donchaknow."

Taylor sighed. "Is it?"

"So then," the old man went on, "I, we were sitting down to dinner and I asked my mother if I might invite this young girl to come to visit, come up from St. Thomas, dow–"

"Which is down in the Virgin Islands?" Taylor offered.

And the children come and go, don't you know.

"Well, I musta done something right," the old man smiled,"cause she ended up staying for eleven weeks!"

"Tsat right..."

"And she ended up staying for about eleven weeks, and went to, she had ten sets of aunts and uncles to visit here in the States, which she went to visit."

Taylor, at a loss to keep up with this random storytelling pattern, countered, more to stall than to understand."Went to see her aunts and uncles, did she?"

"Well, she had ten sets here in the States, then we, so then we decided to get married, donchaknow, and we moved out to Oregon, and then about fourteen years later..."

WHOA!! Taylor's mind objected. UNCLES MARRIED WHAT FOURTEEN OREGON AUNT YEARS LATER WHAT? WHO? DONCH-WHAT?

"And they're off!!!"
"Step right up, ladies and gentlemen..."
"Make it go real fast..."
"For my next trick..."
"Hey, wait for me, guys, wait for me!"

Which the old geezer (geyser) failed to pick up on...

"I said to her that we, I decided we ought to go back to Europe...have you ever been to Europe, young man?"

HAVE I EV ... Taylor thought manically. *YOU JUST ASKED ME THAT!!!*

"Yes," Taylor stated flatly. "Six times. Four times as a military advisor for President Coolidge, once on the lam from Federal agents for smuggling cheap wines into France, and the last ti--"

"Well," the old man countered, "we thought as how we might take the car with us, with the family, cause the wife had said what will we do with the kids, donchaknow, an' I said well, we take them on with us, and the wife agreed, back when we went to Europe, donchaknow."

Taylor still seemed to see this 'donchaknow' as some kind of carrot on a stick, inviting commentary.

Idiot.

"How many kids did you ha–"

"Well, we found out that we could take the car with us to Europe, it was a seven-passenger Cadillac, and we decided to take it with us and the family to Europe, donchaknow, and we took it with us for $565, which was..." he paused, then found his place, "...was, us, which was cheaper than renting one, donchaknow."

"I don't think I've ever seen a seven-person Cadilla–," the Idiot began, before cutting himself off in a flash of instant intellect.

"Eighty-five hundred dollars," the white-lidded museum caromed away, "which wasn't bad for a bunch, that's all we spent, the five of us to travel around Europe for four months in a seven-passenger Cadillac, donchaknow, and they would ask me in Europe, they would say, 'Was fur auto ist das?' and I would say, 'Diese ist ein Amerikanische Volkswagen,' heh-heh, donchaknow, and they got a big kick out of that. Heh-heh."

The gentleman smiled as he remembered telling and telling and telling, Taylor supposed, his little joke to his new German friends. Taylor could visualize the raised eyebrow, the upturned lip of the old man's German victims, entirely unamused. He could imagine German villagers rushing around, calling emergency town meetings to demand the end of NATO.

All the while, the old man's white eyebrows danced up and down in one of those Don't-you-get-it expressions.

Taylor got it. And ran with it. "American Volkswagen, huh? That was a good one, probably got you a good kick, or two, out of that?"

Suddenly, Taylor's jaw dropped, realizing that he, without warning, had managed to finish a complete sentence.

The old man seemed to realize this as well. His expression changed. He looked over his shoulder at the door, his shoulders bunching, and then, uncertainty suddenly clutching him in a clamp of confusion, he spoke.

"Well," the old man said through grim lips, "I told my wife I'd meet her in fifteen minutes, an' it's been a few longer than that, ayuh, but she's not come in here yet, so maybe I'll just sit a bit longer, donchaknow, take off this jacket, if you don't mind, son."

Taylor was subdued by his guest's sudden discomfort. "Certainly, Sir, just make yourself right at ho..."

He stopped and looked at the old man. Their eyes met.

The old man had one sleeve of his jacket off his shoulder already, and then he clicked slightly to a stop, just a dim but pointed pause, before quickly pulling the jacket back up and on. He looked at Taylor, then his eyes began to glisten with tears of embarrassment. He saw Taylor's eyes, over-wide with unbelieving horror, Taylor's eyes riveted to the aged skin just below the short sleeve of the old man's shirt.

In a bolt of frightening clarity, Taylor realized why this hoary old man had seemed to flit around and about these stories of his, why the old man hadn't seemed completely fettered to the confines of the ground but able to circle in and out of his tales, with just a slight bit of the erratic. Say, oh

OH DEAR GOD, PLEASE NO

just about one-fifth of the erratic.

Taylor's mind danced backwards as if his jaw had been shattered. Surely he had not seen ("they would clip just a bit off one wing") what his eyes told him he had seen ("they couldn't clip too much") just below the old man's shirt sleeve.

The seasoned old man's head drooped toward the floor. His mouth moved, opening and closing, as if inspecting his words before they flew out in some ("just slightly erratic") remark.

"Just a little scar I picked up," he muttered, just audibly enough for Taylor to hear, just loud enough to turn Taylor's spine to ice. "A bet I lost once, donchaknow, in a chartered... private car on a train, doncha--"

Taylor's mouth snapped shut to curtain his clamping teeth, grinding his upper jaw into his lower to contain the scream. The shudder got away though, got clean away, and he shivered all too visibly in front of the old (crippled?) man. Taylor saw the clip, the horribly precise clip of flesh missing from above the man's elbow. Taylor could see a triangle of his store's carpet showing through at an obscenely untrue angle, peering from a place where no light should have been able to pass.

The neatly surgical reality of the sight sent sparks splaying through Taylor's skull, as two armies in his brain fought to deny, or worse, to confirm the horrid thoughts that skittered back and forth.

In a flash, Taylor saw pigeons and pheasants, flying erratically over the lagoons and the darker areas of St. Thomas ("which is down in the Virgin Islands, donchaknow?"), abruptly changing course, changing, changing, changing...

...he saw coarse and far too drunk men in a private train car, hooting and howling at the perverse wager they had just made...

...he saw a verbose and spark-eyed man in a barely baggy blue suit, too drunk to aim at the pigeons, the live pigeons in Florida...

...he saw a group of men, more like a coven than a hunting party ("they would bet on just about anything 'tal, donchaknow"), silently carrying out the terms of their hellish wager...

...he saw a natty, confused, wounded aging man, ellipsing through the unpaved and less-traveled streets of St. Thomas...

Taylor knew he was going to scream.

A buzzer seemed to explode in Taylor's head, scattering legions of intentionally wounded birds and gamblers around a great green Christmas bow inside his bruised mind.

The buzzer sounded very familiar, but much too loud. Then his eyes were slapped by a shrill searching diamond of reflected sunlight, drilling towards him at sunlight's relentless pace. He blinked hard, opened his eyes and looked up. The front door of his store, here on the last day of the month, had opened (so that was the loud buzzer). A car windshield was reflecting sunlight directly into his eyes (so that was the diamond drill). Silhouetted in the door of Taylor's store was a woman he had never seen.

But, crazily, Taylor immediately knew who she was...

She spoke. "Winton, are you in here? I'm ready to go... Winton?"

The old man, bright and ancient eyes watering, so very tired, touched his hat with his hand and looked at Taylor, looked straight through him. He spoke. "Coming, dear."

He turned to go, slightly erratic, just so very slightly erratic, winding down the aisle to meet with the brown woman looming at the door.

The waves and oceans, they ebb and flow
Birds here are circling, unsure where to go
For the fathers have clipped their wings just so
And the children come and go, don't you know.

The Misinformation Superhighway

All My Friends Are Plural

(What's a synonym for 'antonym?')

I finally made the switch from English. Now, I speak, like, American and stuff.

What? Get out. Like, you too?

Dude. That's, like, trippy.

What are we doing to ourselves? We've been given this fine, rich, beautiful language, and we're all, like, so trashing it and stuff!

And why would we want to make things more difficult? Heaven knows, good old across-the-big-pond English is hard enough, without our American attempts to creatively balkanize it. I mean, let's face it. You can't *learn* English; you have to *memorize* it. Yes, there *are* rules, but for every rule, there are, like, 116 exceptions, and exceptions to those exceptions. And the exceptions have no pattern; they make no sense at all.

I can ask for "a hot dog," but I'm supposed to recall "an historical moment." No! No, I won't do it. Shut, like, up and stuff.

Is it "this is a group?" Or "these are a group?" Depends on who(m) you ask. Both are allowed...sometimes. But you can get tossed out of very nice restaurants for saying "the group are here," especially if it are (or they is) a group of people with tongue tattoos.

Men buy a pair of pants, but women buy one bra (some, not even that many). We don't cut our grasses, or get our hairs cut, but we brush our teeth, unless we have tongue tattoos. (If we floss our teeth, that qualifies as an historic moment.)

Pronunciation's no walk in an park, either. Here, the rules just flat give up. When faced with pronunciation, the rules just whip out the rice mat and commit ceremonial suicide. It all simply has to be memorized.

You might think spelling would offer some kind clues to pronunciation. Yeah, right. Consider this list, out loud, unless you're standing by yourself in front of a psychiatrist: thought, though, through, tough, bough, ought, drought.

See what I mean? It's just cruel. I don't know how such nonsense happened, but obviously there was a committee involved.

And then there's the issue with people's surnames. Some seem plural, some not. Why? I have friends with last names like Jones and Williams, but I have other friends with last names like Carter, Johnson, Landau-Smythe, and one old college roommate who had to change his to "Doe."

(well, he told *us* he had to) Why the difference? What, please, are the rules? Have you ever met anyone named Tom Jone? Or Ted William? And you've probably never met anyone named Jimmy Carters or Don Johnsons, either, although Don's cousin, Howard, runs a pretty nice hotel chain.

Again - why? Someone needs to look into this. Some vocabulary aficionado needs to take charge, maybe apply for a federal research grant, if the government has any money left after funding all that vital, economy-stimulating research on the effects of cocaine on the sex habits of monkeys.

If you need to locate a vocabulary aficionado (literal translation: that kid in grade school who ate lots of lunches by himself), just grab a crossword puzzle and stand upwind. They are intensely fond of crossword puzzles, especially if they're masochistic aficionados, or don't have, like, jobs and stuff.

Crossword fans are champions of the "synonym." (literal translation: trying to impress women by saying "Fancy an eft, mon cheri?" instead of "Hey babe, ever eat a salamander?") Crossword fiends can quickly be spotted simply by waiting for them to start twitching. In any standard social situation, just casually employ some common word, and wait. It won't take long. The crosswordiacs are so full of synonyms that they can't stand it until they let one fly.

Crossword puzzles provide four major benefits to mankind:

1) They provide single people with an instant dinner companion.
2) They provide crossword-o-philes with the opportunity to use words that just don't come up that often, like "snood" and "aglet" and "eft" and "permanent tax cut."
3) They allow people to smile and call their boss an idiot without getting fired, simply by taking advantage of synonyms they've picked up from working crossword puzzles, such as "ament" or "jack-pudding" or "gobe-mouches" or "inscrutablix" or "mooncalf" or "clueless quasi-literate pond scum" or "ego-emasculating corporate troll." (literal translation: I hope, someday, I catch you unaware and confused in a dark alley, you career-mangling credit-sucking-vampire)
4) They serve as a magnet to attract members of an odd cult, who see you working a crossword puzzle in restaurants and other public places, walk right up, and utter the same, secret, arcane, cult pass-phrase: "You do them things? I can't do them things."

If you're already a crossword addict, you probably know that the ones posted daily in the New York Times get progressively harder, from Monday to Sunday. Monday's is clever and challenging, Sunday's is vicious and sadistic. If the New York Times' weekly crossword puzzles were a collection of scary monsters, they might line up something like this:

Monday: Godzilla

Tuesday: Lorena Bobbit

Wednesday: Dick Cheney

Thursday: that guy at the grocery who stands in front of the canned vegetables, bitterly muttering at somebody you can't see

Friday: Hannibal Lector

Saturday: your dentist, if he was insane, and full of drugs, and had convinced himself that you killed his favorite dog, named Dick Cheney

Sunday: Rahm Emanuel

If you're not yet a crossword fan, let me give you a little tip before you take the plunge. The people who create crossword puzzles are very, very evil (sadistic, ruthless, career politician). They are a vile coven of lunatic literati with a laser-like focus on finding puns, obscure word usage and archaic cross-references. They live to dream up brutally-obtuse hints that are so evil that any polite Romance Language nation would quickly queue them for religious excommunication.

And the most vile transgression of the crossword puzzle-maker is the dreaded invention known as the "var."

This little nastiness involves the crossword's creator just making up words. Just. Making. Them. The. Heck. Up.

As a seasoned crossworder, you understand that "var" means "misspelled." So this means that the puzzle's author has intentionally included some incorrectly-spelled word, just so it would fit in their ghastly game grid. That's just wrong.

But that's not enough for these dark Crossword-Puzzle-Creating Spawn. Nay, nay. The spawn take it a step further, coming up with clues like "ancient Indo-American canoe used between 5 and 6pm, but only by one-armed aboriginal Leopard God priests named 'Ngobo al Corsair' (var)."

There ought to be a law.

So let's save English, America. Let's all get together (collaborate, cooperate, join forces) and clean up our act (succeed, win, bring home the bacon, snootily reject lots of other people). Let's not lose this precious gift (endowment, kindness, inheritance, out-of-control generational-theft welfare).

And if you'd like to read more about the future of language in America, *linea dos, por favor.*

useless.com

(Information superhighway? Maybe. But there are still potholes.)

Not long ago, a Facebook "friend" gonged a frantic warning klaxon, advising everyone to rush to a certain website, because that dastardly website might be displaying <gasp> your phone number and address!

Back in "the day," this was known as a phone book.

After I shook off the heinous horror, and changed my phone number, I thought a visit to the vile website might provide, at worst, a harmless diversion and, at best, a target for my Mother-Theresa-like weekly commentary.

On both counts, the website delivered. In spades.

Now, I won't disclose the name of this website, because I'm furiously averse to being sued. I lack that recessive gene that equates "vacation of a lifetime" with "extended time in prison, starring as the dance partner of a very large man in a red cape." But the aforementioned website is so utterly useless that I hate to deny you, gentle reader, the opportunity to visit. So let's imagine that this is a website whose address begins with "www" and ends with "com" (including all the appropriate, obligatory dots), and I'll try to strew a few clues, cleverly hidden within this story. Fair enough? Okay, let's begin.

S) So I visited the offending website, which offers to lay out lots of information about anybody for whom you search. I searched for myself, which wasn't a hard decision, since I've been doing that for over 50 years now. Sort of.

And the website did find me. Sort of. But...

P) Prior to letting me search, of course, the website offered the standard, boilerplate disclaimers, like the data is "not guaranteed to be 100% accurate." There's your first clue that these people are useless. Data is either accurate, or it is inaccurate. You can't be 58% accurate. In life, some things either are so, or are not so. You can't be partly pregnant. You can't be kinda perfect. It's not possible to sorta like (or sorta hate) Glenn Beck. You can be almost home; you cannot be almost human (unless you're in Congress). Consider the Marx Brothers, or Monty Python. You're either in or you're...

O) Out.

But let's get back to the useless website. I looked myself up, at the address I know for a fact is my correct address, where I have lived, by myself, since I bought the new house a little over 3 years back. And I discovered some surprises. According to the crack research department at Useless, there are 3 people living in my house, which was built 15 years ago. And the real...

K) Kicker is this: my house (according to Useless) has no central heat or air, and is in a "below average" neighborhood, but its estimated value is still over one million dollars. Useless says I don't have a fireplace (yes, I do). Useless informs that I have no interest in politics (wrong), I subscribe to magazines (wrong), and I research investments (you have no idea how wrong). In an odd moment of clarity, Useless does admit that I may have a swimming pool, or I may not. They just don't know.

According to Useless, there are 17 Barry Parhams in the United States, and...

E) Every one of them lives in a "below average" neighborhood. Useless confirms that I have 4 available photographs, none of which are actually me, although a Barry Parham living in Lyman, South Carolina, looks EXACTLY like me. In fact, based on the pronouncements from Useless, my name is not Barry.

Oh, yeah. According to the gang at Useless, there's...

O) One more bit of news. I'm black.

But other eyes, apparently, are mining the data at Useless and are making decisions accordingly. The Census challenged my responses, and the IRS sent round a very large man in a red cape. Thinking quickly, which is not my strongest point, I took advantage of some tax status loopholes. I married myself, and then we adopted myself. I'm now the first single guy in history to be in an interracial marriage. Now I belong to 27 distinct minorities, and have my own Congressman (his name is Hillary Mgobo Juarez Convictowitz, a Yankees fan from a Havana shtetl, affecting a Wall Street-inflicted limp and packing an Arizona-threatened work visa).

After learning this new news about myself, I realized I needed some broad-based advice, so I organized a meeting. I invited selected friends, the 3 rent-ducking rat-bait dastards hidden in my house and, given my new heritage, the NAACP.

One of my attending friends cajoled that Useless just collects info (or simply makes it up), hoping you'll subscribe to their fee-based "tell me more" service, which allows you access to even deeper levels of even more utterly useless, nonsensical non-facts. In other words, no big deal. Don't worry about it.

I think he's just saying that because I'm black.

Sex and Free Money

(Observations on obsessions, politics, and pretzels)

Okay, I only said that to increase my internet search rankings. Now let's move on to today's real topic: How To Choose The Right Mustard.

Okay, just kidding. But beginning this column with the words "sex" and "mustard" is going to seriously skew somebody's internet searches.

Or not.

In fact, as part of my exhaustive research for this column, while my automatic garage door closed, I actually did an internet search for sex AND mustard. And in under a second, the search engine had returned over 1,900,000 results.

One of the search results recommended that I dive in to an article to learn more about South American Population Density and Pollinator Behavior, but I see no reason to drag disgraced South Carolina politicians into this. Moving on...

Nearly 2 million results! Whew. Good thing I didn't search for sex and hot sauce. That could've spun my computer into a weeping jag.

Actually, it wouldn't surprise me in the least to discover that, on any given day, millions of people search the internet for sex and mustard. Maybe these miscreants are mustard aficionados, or fast-food savants. Maybe they're simply shopping: maybe they're members of that nomadic nation who staff the food booths at migratory county fairs, people who for some unknown reason are all named Art Carney, and who all seem to know somebody called "The Snake Lady."

And now the government's urging us to turn in our neighbors if they mention "fish." So before they discover that I dared utter both "mustard" and "sex," let me wrap this up, lest the White House's ever-watchful Opinion Police flag me as unfit, or worse, a potential Cabinet nominee.

What is happening to our country? We're positively obsessed with mustard! Every other day, we hear of some new public figure, proudly announcing that they are coming out of the pantry. Several city and state governments will now pay for their occasionally civil employees to get condiment-change operations – at taxpayer expense!

Recently, a US Senator was arrested in a public restroom. His unique interpretation of his Constitutional duties involved tapping out secret condiment codes on the stall walls, hoping to discuss mustard with like-minded voters.

At first blush, I admit that I found that news hard to believe. But then these are the same elected officials who chastised auto execs for flying their own private jets to

Congressional hearings, and then snuck a line item into America's defense budget to buy ... ready? ... their own private jets.

Sharing mustard with total strangers is not really likely to embarrass such fiends, is it? Anyone who's that hopelessly two-faced must, at least once a week, listen to the wrong face and put their clothes on backwards.

Even your most mundane family activities are assaulted by this condiment craze. Should you make a plan for a familial evening at the local cinema, you have to nimbly navigate the theater's lobby, averting your children's eyes from monstrous, full-color 3-D adverts that luridly lure you and yours towards the movie version of the unsubtly suggestive cable TV hit, "Mustard In The City."

And it doesn't end there. Oh, no. To add insult to penury, you still have to deal with the villains running the concessions stand:

You: I'd like four small sodas, two small popcorns and a pretzel.

Spike-Haired-Person-In-A-Mauve-Smock: That'll be sixty-seven thousand dollars.

You: Will you take a post-dated check?

Spike: Would your daughters like some mustard?

[sounds of a scuffle]

Security Guard: SIR! Release the concessions guy! DO IT NOW!

But remember, America - this fetid fascination with food is nothing new. Keep that in mind, the next time you're idling at a stop light and a voice from the next car croons:

"Excuse me. Do you have any Grey Poupon?"

Truth in (spite of) Advertising

(How to survive a bad economy, if you don't mind the bad karma)

America, times are tough. Hardly a news flash, that. But worry not: opportunity knocks!

Ever considered a career in the exciting field of product advertising? Well, here's your chance!

To get started, take our patented Careers In Advertising quiz below. For each common 'buzz phrase,' just pick the best verbiage to complete the sales pitch.

Good luck!

Our patented process

- ensures the highest quality
- actually applies to an entirely different product
- was 'liberated' from our competition

But you better hurry, because this sale

- definitely ends Monday at midnight
- is based on admittedly dodgy business practices
- will be followed immediately by our next sale

With our unconditional guarantee

- there's absolutely no risk to you
- you can wrap a medium-sized fish
- and a dime, you'd have ten cents

Have your credit card handy

- and call now!
- and hurry up, because our employees are dangerously over-medicated
- because we're standing in an alley, working out of a car trunk

Stock up now, and save!

- Call now!
- This offer can't last forever!
- Limit one.

Operators are standing by!

- Call now!
- These operators can't stand forever!
- Remember, we're in an alley. We can't afford chairs.

After over 5,000 bariatric surgeries

- I've discovered the secret to successful weight loss
- I finally remembered to finish up with sutures
- I'm really sore

These prices are insane!

- So hurry in and save!
- Which explains why our owner is wearing a drool bib.
- But they're an absolute beacon of sanity compared to our "fine print."

Independent scientific studies conclude

- that our product beats the competition!
- that there are zero side-effects!
- that you can get an independent scientific study to say pretty much anything.

We're proud to display the "Made in the USA" tag on every product we sell!

- Buy American and save!
- To order your own "Made in the USA" tags, call 1-800-HOT-WARE.
- Well, yeah, USA does stand for "Unregulated Sweat-shop in Angola," but let's not niggle.

For a limited time, we'll throw in a second Puff-Master Stem-Cell Plunge Monkey for free!

- You just pay shipping!
- Which gives you some idea of our huge profit margins on this crap.
- Amazing. We say 'you just pay shipping' and you people still think it's free. It just boggles the mind.

How can we offer prices like this?

- We buy direct from the factory!
- We more than make it up on the 'shipping.'
- We stole this merchandise!

Side-effects, though rare,

- may include nausea and mild headaches
- may include organ failure and violent convulsions
- may cause you to explode on public transportation

Some restrictions may apply.

- Visit our website for details.
- Which is like saying some of the ocean may be a bit damp.
- And if you actually FIND any relevant details on our website, we'll dance naked during half-time at the Super Bowl.

But wait! There's more!

- If you act now...
- As part of this special TV offer...
- Cause if you've heard all this bilge and you're still listening, you'll probably buy a bunch of this other garbage, too.

After completing the quiz, mail it to our Customer Service Liaison, Aaron Drivel. Please include your name, home address, a brief description of your children's phobias, and a signed, blank personal check. We'll take it from there!

We'll review your career potential, and then arrange some off-shore details that needn't concern you. Please allow 6-8 weeks, or fifteen-to-life, depending. (attorney not included)

Remember: our success depends on you! So call now!

And if you have any questions, you can count on Aaron Drivel.

Potted Meat & the Bad Guys

(How 31,000 years of technology plan to seriously screw up your weekend)

If you're less than 4 decades old, you probably don't remember a world where spam didn't come in an email. Way back then, spam only appeared in a can, or in a Monty Python sketch.

This year, the Internet turned 40. Can you believe it? It's true. The Internet was born in 1969. Very few of us can remember a time when there was no Internet. Of course, given everything else that we were up to in 1969, it's a minor miracle that we can remember anything at all.

But that's another story.

Imagine it. 40 years ago, in a secret government lab underneath Al Gore's house, the very first digital message was sent from one computer to another. Of course, it had a typo. And the second computer never received the message, because it bounced, rejected as spam.

Nevertheless, history had been made. Within the hour, eight-year-old Barack "Barry" Obama had been awarded the Nobel Prize for Computer Science, and Joe "Joe" Biden had leaked the lab's location to the press. Later that afternoon, a government clerk named Elwood Pangorn became the first person in history to be fired for surfing the web during business hours.

Legend tells us that this first-ever message was a simple transmission of a simple phrase: "LO." Of course, legend also tells us that foul, vicious blood-sucking creatures, undead ghouls who take whatever they want from everyone they encounter, once roamed the mountains of Transylvania, and the icy cubicles of the IRS. But that's another story.

According to my exhaustive research, while microwaving a spam-filled Hot-Pocket, the first internet message ever sent was this: "Please forward this joke to eight other people, as soon as we invent six more computers. LOL!"

These days, it's hard to comprehend what life was like before the Internet. We had to manually search for information and knowledge by reading buks, or bukes, or books, or whatever they used to call those little rectangular things. To communicate with our neighbors, friends and family, we had to use the telephone, or in extreme cases, actually stand in front of them and talk. Frightening idea, huh?

To circulate a petition, we had to don white wigs, hop on a horse, and gallop around at midnight, yelling our message of solidarity until we got shot by the enemy or, equally likely, by our own side. We actually had to use envelopes and stamps to share pictures of clothing-challenged Scandinavian women with a severe hormone imbalance.

Spam was canned meat, a virus was a cold, a worm was bait, and "Trojan" was a word you rarely heard uttered within 2 miles of a fundamentalist church.

Nobody had ever heard of carpal tunnel. It was practically impossible for deposed third-world dictators to contact you, offering to transfer their "entirely fortune" to your "bankness" account, in return for one, good, solid English grammar lesson. Google was the surname of a cartoon character. And LOL was either a typo or a secret government program underneath Al Gore's house.

Was it a better time? Or worse? I'm not sure. I'll google it and post the results on YouInnerTube.

Initially, the Internet was a military project, conjured during the paranoid days of the Cold War, created so that if there ever was a global thermonuclear war, we would still be able to receive irritating calls cajoling us to switch long distance companies. Unfortunately, nefarious agents from the Worldwide Communist Threat (The Bad Guys) co-opted the technology, and proceeded to make us interminably stupid, step by step, simply by getting us to send each other the same joke about 418 schlocktillion times.

Seems to be working.

It was late in 1990 when the very first public web page was created. By some counts, there are now so many web pages that it would take the average interminably stupid person 31,000 years to stare at every single page for

1 minute, and somebody that reads this is gonna try it, and I'm pretty sure that I once worked for that guy.

And now, LOL and Behold, the World Wide Web is practically indispensible. We have things like Facebook, which is some kind of mind-altering drug (probably created by The Bad Guys in 1969). Facebook makes people share stuff like "**I'm going to bed now**" and "**r u bored? me 2! LOL!**" and "**I'm almost ready to prepare to begin getting ready to leave work.**" And then there's Twitter, with its brutal 140-character limit that causes people to post shorthand-y stuff like this: "**Must! #stategov #allthat @ LeLe @nochance bit.ly/GvwSeK - So much 4 u! LOL.**"

I'm pretty sure I worked with that guy, too.

Of course, the Internet would never have made it past the white-board stage without the computer itself. So let's take a quick moment to acknowledge those visionaries, those hardy pioneers: IBM, who invented the first personal computer (the PC); Apple, who invented the first cool computer (the Mac); and Microsoft, who invented the memory leak (the Loud Swearing).

The Internet. Overall, it's an amazing history. In 1972, there were only 2,000 humans online (oddly enough, all named Elwood). This year, over 1.6 billion of us are out there, sending the same two jokes back and forth, back and forth, back and forth. Moreover, for those long weekends, we now have 31,000 years of available reading. And, perhaps most amazing of all, the Internet has been around for forty years now, and Congress still hasn't figured out how to tax it.

31,000 years. Better get busy. And when you're done, America will *still* be in debt.

But that's another story. LOL.

Communication's Swiss Army Knife

(How to win friends, influence people, and conquer Russia)

According to history, the first email ever transmitted was sent from Thomas Edison, and contained the simple phrase,"Watson, RU their. LOL"

It bounced.

Since that fateful day, email and its caffeine-crazed cousin, instant messaging, have burrowed their way into the fabric of American communication. In fact, for many people, email has taken precedence over other, more common aspects of daily life, like personal hygiene, or being literate. Checking email is often the first thing, and the final thing, people do each day. Some people will check their email before they even get dressed for the day, and if that image doesn't spoil your breakfast, then you're probably reading this naked.

Similarly sobering is the self-important value that some people assign to their emails. You may know some of these people: they'll send you an email and then call to tell you, "I just sent you an email." Sad, isn't it?

And then there are those ego-the-size-of-the-Hindenburg people you run into in public places (because you weren't quick enough to hide) who ask, "Did you get my email?" They seem to think you never get emails from other humans, certainly not any emails worth reading. In their minds, you just sit in front of your computer, day after day, possibly wearing clothing, eagerly, hungrily waiting for them to forward you another joke.

But in fact, we all get emails, all the time, from all kinds of people and places and companies, including many that actually exist. So by now, we all know the common, humdrum functions of email. Let's review a few:

- I'd Like To Teach The World To Laugh: This is the primary function of email - to forward jokes from one place to another. Prior to the invention of email, I'm not really sure how jokes ever made their way around the planet. Back in "the day," I don't remember people forwarding me the same joke 300 times using the fax machine. Maybe universal joke dispersal was why Eisenhower commissioned the interstate highway system.
- The Olan Mills Syndrome: Use email to share your exceptional photographic talents. Trust me - nothing excites your friends and co-workers more than getting that email with the "Here are some photos I wanted to share with you" subject line.
- The Artistic Gang-Hug: Coming in a close second to the Olan Mills samples are emails that announce

"You have got to see this!" or "This is the most beautiful thing ever!" No, I don't, and no, it isn't.

- Guarding The Global Intellect: Everybody loves it when they get an email, challenging them to "take this IQ test!" Be sure to include your own score on the test, and be sure to insist they copy their score to several dozen friends, so that "something magical will happen on your screen!" I don't know about your screen, but if you keep this up, something magical will definitely happen to your several dozen friendships.
- Workplace Ergonomics 101: When people forward you an email that begins with 217 vertical miles of "forwarded" email headers and other useless garbage before you get to the actual message, don't think of it as a interruption; think of all that scrolling as a handy wrist exercise for your "mouse" hand. But to keep things honest, I should mention that scientists have recently proved that the actual value of an email's message is inversely proportional to its length.

Yeah, I know. Right now, you're probably saying, "What's your point? I know all this. Why am I sitting here freezing to death reading what I already know? I'm gonna go get dressed."

Ah, but email has many more uses: more entertaining, esoteric and sinister uses, like buying a bride from Russia or a prescription drug from Canada. You just have to learn to think outside the inbox. You just have to be creative, like you were with your taxes or when filling out the Census form. Here are some handy ideas about how to get more out of your email experience:

- Captain Sparky & The Dawn Patrol: Did you ever consider that you can use email to find out if somebody is awake? Think about it. Like me, you probably have at least one friend who, at some point every morning, starts sending you emails. Every morning, every day, like Sisyphus. Obviously, your friend is up, out of bed, and busily forwarding yesterday's jokes. Of course, they may or may not be clothed. Some things are best not etc., etc.
- Virtual Immortality: When you get a useless spam message from someone you don't know, be sure to take advantage of that handy "remove me" link. Once you click that link, the slimeball sender will know for certain that your email address is, actually, your real, valid email address. From that point on, you'll get billions of emails from them (and from billions of other slimeball companies, because Slimeball Company #1 will sell them your email address). This will continue for the rest of your natural life, and for several years after. (Think I'm kidding? Slimeball emails will follow you into the afterlife. Recall, if you will, a passage from the New Testament: "Lead us not into temptation, but deliver us some email.")
- The First 300 Cuts Are The Deepest: One of the best ways to permanently damage a personal or professional relationship is to pack your email message with subtle sarcasm and biting jest-filled jabs. Smi-

ley Faces aside, it's practically impossible to successfully communicate sarcasm in an email message. So do it every chance you get, and in no time at all, you'll be released from the restraints of gainful employment and interpersonal companionship – you'll be just free to sit at home every day, checking your email and freezing to death!

- Corporate Espionage: Picture it. Management has scheduled a 10:30 meeting, to discuss cutting costs by getting rid of everybody's chairs. Using your personal Crack-Pod-Device-Berry-Phone-i-Thingy, record the entire meeting and then broadcast it via email to all non-management personnel. For extra credit, use Blu-Tooth technology to make it look like the email was sent from somebody else. For personal security, choose somebody smaller than you.
- Demand & Supply: Remember those emails with 217 miles of "forwarded" headers? Don't delete them just yet; instead, harvest those thousands of email addresses and sell them to a slimeball company! Or use them to create your own contact database and form your own grass-roots political party! With a core constituency of email addicts, you're sure to have no shortage of misspelled signs for your rallies!
- Culling The Herd: Rather than waiting around to get a virus from software, it's much more efficient to just start clicking attachments in emails sent from people you don't know. Give special attention to emails that contain phrases like "Are these pictures of you from that party?" or "I are having so hot for you."

There's another email feature I could include in this handy list, but it really deserves its own discussion, because it's in a class of its own. Let's talk about this one later, but for now, I give you three words: Blind Carbon Copy.

Trust me. It's absolutely delicious, what this thing can do. This is the monster under the bed. This is the room under the stairs. This is Rasputin.

Email me. We'll talk.

Queasy Rider

(Junk mail, bad hobbies, and a permanent limp)

Yeah, yeah, it's true. I got arrested. As it turns out, it's against the law to drive on the freeway naked. Who knew?

Recently, by an odd and vile coincidence, I received three marginally-enticing invitations in the mail. No, not those regularly-delivered over-sized envelopes screaming "Open Immediately!" -- each containing one more "Your Last Chance!" offer to use the "secret key!" on my "personal awards ticket!" to "buy a new car!" for "below dealer invoice!" Apparently, many car dealers make a habit of selling cars for less than they paid for the car, and how they manage to turn a profit is "none of my business!" The dealership always assumes, of course, that my "bank" will lend me some "money" which, these days, is "not bloody likely."

And no, I'm not talking about the daily carpet-bombing barrage of offers to switch calling plans, or insurance plans, or credit cards, or home security systems, or brokers, or life partners, or deities. Nor do I mean the endless advisories from follicle-challenged Watergate-era felons insisting that I invest in gold before sundown or else, or all the concerned contacts from various lawyers, advising me to check myself carefully for injuries or asbestos stains. And

I'll brush past the pile of "Grand Opening" fliers from the eight dozen or so Chinese restaurants that spring open each week, that for some inscrutable reason are all named after a "Garden" or a "Panda" (or both).

No, no. Nothing so pedestrian as that.

The first teaser was my weekly lure from the Armed & Ancient Republican Party (the AARP). Not that it's unusual for me to receive AARP mailings. My, that's a persistent bunch! But given their massive marketing costs and my insouciant refusal to assimilate into their little Borg Cube collective, they are now perched at the point of desperation. This latest mailing mixed short-lived restaurant discounts and free golf with morbid mortality statistics and the veiled threat of Borg-induced bowel issues.

The second invite was from a politician, pleading with me to send him some money, so he could continue his heroic stand against the nefarious bad guys and the evil unions (Brotherhood Spawn, Local 666), so he could go get re-elected, so that ... I'm not good enough to make this stuff up ... he could continue to fight for term limits.

And then the third item. The one that caused all the trouble. A "coming events" flier from a group of nudist bikers.

Now, in my own defense: on a normal day, I would have tossed such a thing directly into the recycle bin. I mean, a person old enough to be continuously courted by the

AARP does not spend his days rooting about for opportunities to roam the roadways in the company of naked people named Axle Sabbath, Little Endorphin Annie and Senator Boxer. But I wasn't thinking clearly that day, possibly due to a bad decision the night before, involving an Occidental overdose of discounted food at the "Grand Opening" for The Great Wall of Panda Garden Wok Palace and People's Long March Buffet.

And so, that's how I got involved with The Cheeky Riders.

According to their website, The Cheeky Riders originated in 2003, and were then founded in 2004 (not sure how that works, but then, I'm not naked). A couple of years later, the group was purchased and now has an "owner" (for your own peace of mind, don't even dwell on that). Since then, they've grown exponentially, hired a guy (possibly named Anvil Posture) to head up their "expantion," and brought on a "special lady doing membership."

I just bet she is.

The Cheeky Riders sponsor a full, rich calendar of events, including the ever-popular "Get Nekkid" weekend, the nearly lethal Alaskan Nude Cruise, and the nearly legal Leather & Lace Dance. They also have a regularly-scheduled "costume contest," which is confusing, considering their nekkidosity.

On many levels, The Cheeky Riders website is a textbook model for lack of restraint. The web designer was obviously a student of the "use everything, check nothing" school, so the site is rich with blinking text, scrolling marquees, spinning icons, garish colors, sneak-attack sound clips, broken links, missing images, grammar beyond recognition and typos beyond belief.

From a content perspective, I'll just quickly mention their "Our Favorite Tattoos" page, which is not for the squeamish. Remember, these people eschew all attire. They're like Victoria's Secret with no secrets left. There's also a handy link to a "Nudists on the Internet" directory which displays, among other squeam-inducing things, a cartoon drawing of ... I'm not good enough to make this stuff up ... a nude couple playing croquette.

While you're visiting the site, you'll probably want to go ahead and request a "Cheeky Riders" membership application, though you should know that "all applicates are subject to approve." There are membership options for "single" (in case you're single) and "coupe" (in case you're a car or are participating in a misspelled South American junta).

Said membership, be it for singles, subcompacts, or jungle mercenaries, is available on a yearly or lifetime basis (mercenaries are recommended to consider the shorter-term arrangement). Benefits include 20% off the chic Cheeky Riders clothing line, which is an interesting perk, coming from a gang of eventually sunburned nudists. You'll also snag an exclusive Cheeky Riders membership patch, and I've asked a lot of people, and none of them want to ponder where you're supposed to put *that*.

Speaking of stuff to buy, the Cheeky Riders online shopping catalog offers dozens of broken links to, we're guessing, stuff to buy. One link proclaims "By now!" and enquiring minds are waiting to learn how that sentence will end. But fortunately, despite the dearth of unclothed proofreaders, a few choice items are available. Right this very minute, at Cheeky Riders, you can order your very own "Ladies sleeveless ripped front shirt, with clear crystals on edge of rips." Makes the perfect Early Parole gift!

Other equally discerning fashion finds are available at Cheeky Riders, though I noticed that none are available for the petite visitor. The catalog caters to sizes Medium, Large, X-Large, 2XX-Large, Is All Dat You, Fantasy Mother-In-Law, No Really Is All Dat You, and NASA Booster Rocket. Apparently, if you're a "Small," you have only two career options at Cheeky Riders: hors d'oeuvre or hood ornament.

So there I was, wide-eyed and wondering. I'd been granted a view into an alternate universe. My interest in full-body chaffing was piqued (and it was a gorgeous day). But I wasn't quite ready to embrace the entire Cheeky Riders worldview. I'm just that way. I mean, a guy who's made it past age 50 and is still single has to admit to at least a few commitment issues.

As a compromise, I decided to ease into it. To test the waters, as it were. So I shuttered the windows, dimmed the lights, jettisoned the jeans, suppressed a shiver, slathered on some SPF 80, hopped in my new, subcompact South

American insurrection (bought below dealer invoice), and headed for the mall to buy a new croquette mallet.

How invigorating! No more some mere mortal, but a rebel, bold, outbound and unbound! A little chilly, yes, but I scoff at such! Scoff, I tell you! And then, somewhere near the freeway exit, I leaned over to crank up the radio.

Bad idea.

One day, when we both have some time, let's discuss the shortcomings of seat belts. For now, let's just say that seat belt designers, fine ergonomic engineers though they may be, did not take into account the possibility that seat belt wearers might not be wearing anything else. The resulting, uh, discomfort caused me to emit kind of a high-pitched "yip" noise, and then I back-ended the motorbike of a retired AARP lawyer delivering Chinese food.

And that's how I got arrested.

Who knew?

Lord Metatron and the Otter Warden

(Once again, the internet has all the answers. But you should hurry.)

In case you missed last Thursday's galactic conference call, let's start with a simple explanation.

In the root of the Chinese Four Pillar Chart, there is a rat surrounded by two dragons. In the stems of the chart, there is yang fire. The rat is a Water sign; the dragon is an Earth sign. Water, the strongest element, can be found in the rat and the two yang waters. Water and Earth are enemies. The dragons seem to be making plans to eat the rat, which will herald the "Time of No Time," especially for the rat.

See? How obvious is *that*? So now, thanks to the internet, even the most skeptical doubter can clearly conclude that the world will end in 2012.

Still hesitant? Well, maybe you forgot that the Maize God at Chicken Itza's Lower Jaguar Temple has crosses under his armpits, representing the crossing places of the ecliptic and the Milky Way! Ha! *Now* try to deny that we're transitioning from Kali Yuga to Satya Yuga!

So there it is. Time and space are shifting. The planets are aligning, a transitional age approaches, and somewhere out there is one seriously rattled rat. And all of this clearly means that we're moving, astrologically-speaking, into the Age of Aquarius (literal translation: "Rodent Water"). Of course, the Age of Aquarius already made us a nice offer once, back in the '60s, but at the time we were too busy moving into the Age of Puberty to notice.

But time and space are our friends. As Lord Metatron comfortingly intones, "Time exists so that the dumb stuff doesn't all happen at once, and space exists so that it doesn't all happen to you."

According to my research, conducted while I was thinking up anagrams for "Rodent Water," the ancient Mayans measured time in Uinals (literal translation: "Port-O-Let"). 18 Uinals make a Tun, 20 Tuns make a Katun, and 20 Katuns make a Baktun (literal translation: "nearly as long as a Joe Biden speech"). Thirteen Baktuns is known as a "Great Cycle," because by then the Mayans had invented English. And this entire, timeless method of time measurement was known as the "Long Count." (literal translation: "football strategy on third down and short")

Anagram Update: Wade To Trent

The ancient Mayans spent a lot of time staring into space, which often happened when ancient cultures ran around inventing tequila. Venus, for example, was a favorite astrological symbol for the Mayans, who called the little planet "Tlauixcalpantecuhtli." (literal translation: "anagram for Venus after inventing tequila")

The ancient Mayans also invented basketball. On days when they were able to actually stand, they would form teams and try to toss an ancient ball through a round hole in an ornately-carved ring of stone. The captain of the winning team was duly honored (literal translation: "sacrificed to Venus"), which was a bit messy, but fabulous for ancient network ratings, especially during Sweeps Uinal.

Using their calendars, charts, and a wedge of lime, the Mayans calculated that by 2012 we will have gone beyond time, technology, money, and human intelligence as we know it. This clearly explains, for the first time, why the Congressional Health Care Bill doesn't go into effect until 2013.

Anagram Update: Red Ant Tower

I hate to go off on a tangent, but at this point I must mention crop circles, because ... well ... because I must. Hang on. A crop circle known as the "Etchilhampton Grid" was interpreted, by a bloke named Steve, to be a pointer to the year 2012, after Steve discovered that he could fit 3 Mayan calendars in the grid, if he bent one of the calendars. (see "Tequila, Side-Effects Of") Steve's discovery prompted another guy, also named Steve, to point out that the grid correlated with a map called the "Psi Bank Warp and Holonomic Woof." And if you think I'm gonna miss an opportunity to say "Holonomic Woof," then you don't know much about me.

My internet research also unearthed another dude (Steve, again) who has invented a time travel machine, so you can just cut to the chase, nip forward in time, and have a peek at 2012. Steve's blog includes a link to some website where you can "*buy the plans now!*" (literal translation: "there's one born every minute")

Anagram Update: Rotten Wader

The internet tells us what will happen next, and what it will mean. The Sun will be at 0 degrees Capricorn, making an almost exact sextile to Neptune at the beginning of Pisces, which will result in a spiritual experience. Or a loss. Or maybe both.

Well, of *course* it will. What else would you expect from an almost exact sextile at 0 degrees? Tell us something we *don't* know. Lord Metatron comfortingly intoned on *that* one weeks ago.

By the way ... according to the internet, Lord Metatron is the Keeper of the Keys, who lives at the center of the galaxy and is comfortingly adding a love force coloring to the Standing Wave within the folds of Gaia, and I think you'll agree that it's high time somebody did. You can sign up for his monthly conference call for only $25. (see "Bogus Time Machine Scams") Alternatively, Lord Metatron does offer free Manifesting Calls, which is a pretty good deal, since the center of the galaxy generally isn't included in your average extended-area calling plan.

Anagram Update: Torte Drawer

Interestingly, for a conference call that originates in the center of the galaxy, it's scheduled for 8.30pm Eastern Standard Time, leading some theologians to theorize that Lord Metatron may not really reside in the center of the galaxy, but somewhere in the Bronx (the internet adamantly confirms and denies this). But should you miss the call, a transcript is available as a downloadable PDF, and please believe me when I tell you that I am not good enough to make this stuff up.

2012. It's coming. Are you ready? Have you prepared? Do you have enough quarters at hand for the next conference call? Have you even deciphered "Otter Warden" yet?

Internet Update: sadly, The Third Steve's web-link to the "time machine blueprints" is broken.

In my opinion, so is The Third Steve.

Perfect

(Notes on dating and other self-inflicted wounds)

"This time, it will be different."

Count on it, single guy. Count on that shoulder-perching little imp, teasingly muttering.

No matter how terminally single a single guy is, the day is bound to come. The day when endless pizza and unself-conscious scratching in public are just not enough. Some internal biological timer trips, reason is jettisoned, a history of justifiable futility gets ignored, and it's time to try dating again.

This time, it will be different.

True, there's that other nagging little voice shrieking, "NO!" That cautious guardian hovering somewhere near the single guy's wallet (or pineal gland). Doesn't matter. Universal forces prevail ... cosmic forces with a sick, cosmic-sized sense of humor.

This time, it will be different.

No, it won't. But this time, I'm here to help.

Admittedly, I may not be your stellar candidate for Dating Coach of the Year. After all, I'm older than Alaska's statehood, I think Hall & Oates were brilliant, and I still have bangs. But I do include an interesting and fairly unique bullet point in my curriculum vitae. As it turns out, I am America's Penultimate Husband. A surprising number of women that I've dated have married the very next guy they met. Somehow, I became a very useful practice spouse.

So let's proceed to the tactical. For starters, I've put together the following "man seeks woman" personal ad template, that my many "what's the big deal with the toilet seat?" comrades-in-singlehood can post to the ubiquitous dating services available in print media and online.

Single hetero male seeking minimally neurotic, baggage-free, non-ferret-owning female for companionship, dating, and ultimately destructive miscommunication. I enjoy music, dining, and writing odd stories about shrimp, civil servants, and other alien life forms. The ideal candidate will have ten (or more) of her original teeth, and zero (or less) pierced face parts. Please send, for review, an audio tape containing an average-decibel sample of your voice during a heated argument. Active, dues-paying Satanists, the heavily-tattooed, and career politicians need not apply.

Not bad, eh? No? What, too subtle? You see something I've missed? Well, feel free to personalize. Adjust as needed. Maybe you don't write stories about aliens and shrimp.

That's entirely up to you, of course, but if you don't, well, good luck getting a date.

And now for the real goods. As a seasoned single veteran, I've put together this helpful checklist of qualifying / disqualifying characteristics which, any minute now, I'll think up. I may include some additional comments, too, if any occur to me. I don't know yet. That's what puts the "creative" in "creative writing." And remember, it's not like I'm getting paid for this stuff.

Neither the checklist nor my comments are certain to work for you, although they're practically guaranteed to be utterly useless. (That's what puts the "disclaimer" in "legal disclaimer.") Okay, let's get busy:

The Perfect Woman...

- ...will own at least 2 Frank Zappa albums. This not only assures that you're both in a compatible age bracket; it confirms that, as teenagers, you were both equally dazed and confused. Extra credit if she giggles anytime you say "dromadrosis" or "moving to Montana."
- ...thinks delivery pizza and day-old pizza are two of the five food groups. (The other three, of course, being coffee, Chinese takeaway, and two-day-old pizza)
- ...has never been blind-date-pitched by her friends as "she's a real keeper" or "she has a great personality" or "she makes her own clothes."

- ...will have nothing pasted to her car that advertises "I (heart symbol) something." Another common warning sign is "I'd rather be ..." bumper stickers, like "I'd rather be mud wrestling farm animals while under the influence of psychotropic drugs." Pretty good clue, that.
- ...would support binding federal legislation to have ferrets classified as foreign enemy combatants. Now, here, some people will take me to task. "Ferrets aren't evil," they'll say. "Ferrets are cute." Ferrets aren't evil? Have you ever SEEN a ferret? Basically, it's a rat with a zoning variance.
- ...will have a sane amount of beauty products. Check to be sure that her bathroom "body maintenance" cabinet has never been mistaken for a restricted-access laboratory at the Center for Disease Control.
- ...has never sent an "I'm sorry your relative died" email. Research shows that a woman who fires off "condolences" emails will go all Lorena Bobbitt on you at your first toilet seat infraction.
- ...will have reflexes sufficient to protectively duck, should a shoe ever be slung from across the room at the television news. (I'm just saying)
- ...will not have any relatives within a hundred mile radius who have ever shown up at a church wedding wearing a tank top, Bermuda shorts and black stretch socks. Also, be sure to check the relatives for ferret bites.
- ...has never been in a bar, run into an old friend who is an escaped felon, and greeted him with a secret

handshake and the wistful expression, "Hey, Slade. I miss your discipline."

So there you are, single guys. Armed, and warned. In these weird days, caution must be your byword. I once spent three weeks online, chatting up a gorgeous coed named Amber, before I learned that she was actually my old college roommate, Chris.

Now, some will say I'm too picky, and that's why I'm still single. I disagree. I prefer "discerning." And besides, if you've read *this* far and still can't figure out why I'm single, I really don't know what else to say. Maybe, one day, my imp will whisper again.

Once I get over Amber.

Places to Avoid Before You Die

Shrimp and Cocktails

(There's a reason why intelligent life keeps refusing to contact our planet)

Just as predicted, the week ended badly. As of Friday, the pirates still held Houston, the shrimpers were still stuck in the submarine, and Florida's Governor surprised everybody by announcing he planned to run against himself.

On Monday, you'll remember, Somali pirates captured a British Petroleum oil rig off the coast of Louisiana. The Somali pirates held the rig for ransom, which British Petroleum refused to pay, so the pirates scuttled the drilling platform by hitting it repeatedly with a large African parrot. Pet store stocks skyrocketed.

The collapsing oil rig landed on its own umbilical cord, nearly a mile beneath the surface of the Gulf of Mexico, a body of water that recently had illegally migrated to Arizona to enjoy free health care. The fragile cord cracked, spilling millions of petro-dollars into the Gulf. The White House claimed that the incident saved or created 23 million job-shaped oil slicks. Oil stocks skyrocketed.

Eager to accept its civic responsibility for this disaster, British Petroleum started suing obscure companies, a move which the White House claimed saved or created 23 million law schools. Thousands of local shrimpers and fishermen (all named Odephus Tibideaux) appeared in television interviews, demanding BP reimburse them for lost income, and beer money. BP's legal department countered, citing an obscure 1851 court ruling that clearly showed the entire incident to be George Bush's fault.

Public sentiment, however, was on the side of the seafolk, especially after the un-shrimped shrimp population began to grow, and middle-aged shrimp started showing up in the lobbies of Pensacola resort hotels, wearing Bermuda shorts and demanding drink coupons. Clearly, something had to be done. A quick political coalition was formed between Louisiana's senior Senator (Odephus Tibideaux) and the Governor of Mississippi (Medieval Barbour), and thanks to their quick efforts, British Petroleum was designated as "too big to fail." BP stock skyrocketed.

Out-of-work shrimpers negotiated a temporary employment deal with BP, in return for the shrimpers agreeing to, as Odephus Tibideaux described the meeting, "sign here." Then the shrimpers boarded a circa-1851 submarine, made by Halliburton, and headed down to the ocean floor to deal with The Leak. Halliburton stock skyrocketed.

After posting his weekly Twitter address to the nation, the President of the United States flew down to the Gulf Coast. (He didn't take Air Force One; he just flew.) The President met with Odephus Tibideaux and, according to inside sources, nodded knowingly. The White House claimed that, while on the coast, the President performed or created 23 million miracles. In a touching moment of raw emotion, MSNBC kneeled and proposed to the President.

Meanwhile, stymied by America's flawless, impenetrable immigration policy, the Somali pirates sailed directly into downtown Houston where, in a clever early-morning coup, they kidnapped the entire Houston police department at a Dunkin' Donuts. Krispy Kreme stock skyrocketed.

Late Tuesday, the shrimper submariners ran into a snag on the ocean floor when their communication cables got tangled in Geraldo Rivera's moustache, who was on the seabed filming a FoxNews documentary about Jimmy Hoffa, who was deep-sixed in 1851 by George Bush. CNN stock skyrocketed.

Faced with flagging poll numbers, Florida's Governor held a mid-week rally for vacationing shrimp in Pensacola, forming a marsh-roots political movement and promising to provide shrimp an equitable representation in chicken salad. During the rally, according to the White House, the Governor switched or created parties 23 million times, breaking the 1851 record held by the founder of Louisiana, Odephus Tibideaux.

On Thursday, though it did not directly affect the situation in the Gulf of Mexico, Senator Orrin "Booby" Hatch was whisked away for psychiatric evaluation after he interviewed a Supreme Court nominee. According to inside sources, Hatch spent the entire session babbling about a prized flintlock firearm hanging on the wall in his office. Whew. Anti-psychotic drug stocks skyrocketed.

And then it all came full circle. A clever commodities broker spotted all these rising stocks, whipped together an alchemic algorithm, and struck pay dirt. He encoded a message to the submariners, promising them untold riches if they would just "sign here." The local shrimpers, sick to the gills of life on a circa-1851 submarine that wasn't wired for cable, wired their collective savings accounts to the broker.

But the over-eager trader acted poorly. After a few too many celebratory nips at lunch, he wobbled back to his firm and, shortly, he had that undeniable urge to visit the Little Broker's Room. But in his addled condition, he misjudged and entered the firm's computer center. On the wall inside the door were two labeled on-off switches:

1) Lights
2) Global Economic Collapse

Yep. There's the week, explained. As predicted, it ended badly.

World markets went postal. In seconds, fortunes vanished. Vacationing shrimp in Pensacola lost everything. Sarah Palin had to sell her election-cycle shoe collection to Imelda Marcos. Al Gore was forced to pull back and buy only one multi-million dollar home in California. A suddenly destitute Orrin Hatch had to list his precious flintlock on eBay, where it was purchased by an extremely incompetent naturalized American citizen who tried to use it to blow up Times Square.

A furious fiscal ripple resonated across the world's markets, ultimately causing Goldman Sachs to have to buy Greece, an ancient civilization that flourished, even without cable, until it collapsed in 1851, a disaster which we now know was George Bush's fault.

West of Southeast North

(Post-colonial culture, decoded cuisine, and nervous horses)

I'm hearing that the world will end in 2012. That's a little harsh, but hey - if that's what it takes to implement term limits, I'm in.

But after hearing about this ultimate "last call," I thought it best to try some new things. Slow down and savor. Look over some overlooked stuff. Stop buying 2-liter cola. Quit waiting for *Saturday Night Live* to get funny again.

Then, last week, I had occasion to drive from north South Carolina, to south South Carolina, and back again. From the top, down to the bottom, and back up. So since the world was pending ending, I opted to avoid the free-ways and leisurely motor "through the country."

Wow. As the saying goes, "same planet, different worlds."

I drove through one village so small that there was only one light. Not a traffic light, mind you – just this one truck, with a single functioning brake light. During the fes-tive holidays, they park the truck in the square, and citizens take turns pressing and releasing the brake pedal. It's magical. The burg had one store (The Mobile Home Depot). The bank's ATM dispensed change. They had a Commission of Private Works. City Hall was, literally, in a hall. This town was so tiny, they only had 8 McDonalds.

Another city along the way boasts that it's the "Home of Ten Governors," a boast they make about every ten feet. Somewhere, there's an enterprising artisan who makes "Home of Ten Governors" signs, and that is one wealthy artisan indeed. However, with ten preening peer politicians running around loose, you definitely want to avoid their endless, mind-numbing City Council meetings. I understand they're still debating whether or not America should get involved in the War of 1812.

[SIDEBAR] According to my research, all 10 of these Governors apparently had access to excellent maps in their time, since none of them ever ducked out to go hiking and somehow ended up in Argentina.

Deeper along in the country, one fast-food joint's marquee suggested that hungry drivers "TRY OUR NEW." That's it. Just "TRY OUR NEW." Sometimes, I suppose, it's best to ease into marketing.

I drove past another store with two signs by the road, but no signage whatsoever on the building itself. Apparently, the store was actually named "Open Saturday."

[SIDEBAR] As you read along here, be aware that "rural" does *not* mean "dumb." Another diner along the road offered something called a BOGO double cheeseburger. Everybody in that town understood the promising benefits of BOGO. Not me. I supposed it to be some kind of imported meat. It took me two whole days and an intensive internet search to figure out that BOGO meant "Buy One, Get One."

And then there were the hunters. Everywhere. In groups or solo. With hounds or without. But all in full camouflage and all heavily armed.

I'm not a hunter, but I have nothing against hunting. At least hunters seem to respect their prey, which is more than I can say for members of Congress. And hunters never ask you for money. So hunting is fine by me - I'm just not a hunter. What I know about guns is this: you should hold the woody end. That's it.

On one short stretch of highway, I saw seven or eight groups of hunters, all leaning against tricked-out trucks and perfecting their tactics for the next Spittoon Olympics.

One sportsman sat in his truck, leaning out the driver's window, holding what looked like a small, spoked aluminum aerial. Maybe he was tuned in to the Ten Governor Boast-A-Thon. Maybe he was triangulating turkey biorhythms. Or maybe he was sitting alone in a truck, with an antenna and a shotgun, because he was deep-bat-cave barking insane. He was armed, so I didn't ask. I drove on.

A few hundred yards along, I saw a very nervous-looking turkey standing in the soft shoulder, trying to thumb a ride, which is a good trick when you don't have thumbs. The edgy turkey was holding up a fatalistic placard: *Florida or Baste*. Around the next bend was another uneasy bird, announcing its own hard luck story: *Just Got Fired (At). Will Work To Not Be Food.*

But if the world goes on for a million more years, and I'm there for every one of them, nothing will ever top what I saw next - a building bearing this fascinating shingle: "Elite Equine Shavings."

I don't know where to start.

What goes on inside that windowless complex? What do they make, or sell, or ... do to ... what? What does their logo look like? When there's a job opening for staff or middle management, what skills are required? How would one re-rig one's résumé for that plum gig? Could that displaced, jobless, hitchhiking turkey apply?

Exactly what service do they provide at Elite Equine Shavings? Do they sell shaved horses? Have you, personally, ever shopped in vain for a bald horse? If you answered "yes," have you considered therapy? Have you, personally, ever wished for such psychotic, shameless control over any mammal? If you answered "yes," what Congressional district do you represent?

Have the marketers at Elite nosed out some niche, some ignored audience, some clinically disturbed group craving horse shavings? Or are they simply horse barbers? Is this some upscale Mane Salon for that well-groomed horse-about-town? What out-of-date magazines lie about in the lobby for their prancing patrons? *Equine Esquire*? *Better Stables and Gardens*? How much is a hoof manicure?

Is there an epicurean market segment somewhere, clamoring for shaved horse? Do the workers freeze-dry the animal and go at it over time, or do they process a thorough thoroughbred all at once?

I noted that Elite Equine Shavings was situated just next to the local airport, so they can quickly respond to any restaurant facing a horse shavings shortage. Personally, I can't even count the number of times I've been preparing for a high-brow, tony soirée, only to realize at the last minute that I'm fresh out of diced horse. Worry no more! Just add Elite to your speed dial!

[SIDEBAR] There actually is a town called North, South Carolina. Interestingly, it's seventy-five miles from Ninety Six. And North, South Carolina, is 100 miles southeast of Due West.

I know this, because that's where I dropped off the turkey.

There Goes the Neighborhood

(How nice it would be sometimes to just say, "Beam me up, Scotty.")

In this "good grief - what next?" world, we should always look for promise and wonder.

And, as ever, NASA has delivered.

The heroes at NASA have just upgraded the long-laboring Hubble telescope. Although the famous sky-eye has performed well beyond its original specs, it recently suffered from a rare "Irony Overload" when it overheard a partisan politician say, "It's not fair! I don't remember anybody ever questioning George Bush's legitimacy to be President."

No it didn't. The Hubble overheard no such thing. Such a remark would surely set off some kind of pan-galactic logic / anti-logic implosion.

Actually, the Hubble has been working a treat ever since the set-up team noticed they'd missed the next-to-last instruction in the "How To Deploy The Hubble" manual: *Remove lens cap.*

But now, thanks to the new-and-improved Hubble, we've seen grand, glorious images of a distant star, caught in the cataclysm of its final stages – it's dying throes. Majestic and maddening. An amazing display.

And, in a way, such a discovery helps us to recognize our place in this vast cosmos. A TV news crew interviewed one noted physicist, who looked like he was being attacked by his own hair, and the hair was winning. According to the pate-panicked scientist, our own Sun will give up and go dark in exactly 5 billion years, next Thursday. Ironically, ole Sol will snuff out just 8 days before we pay off our national debt.

Obviously, due to the unimaginable distances involved, the Hubble is actually looking into the past. Isn't that wild? Everything the telescope shares with us happened long, long ago, sometime during Dick Clark's childhood.

In fact, the new Hubble has peered so deeply into the endless universe that it actually spotted a crash-proof, virus-free Windows operating system.

No it didn't.

But the Hubble II does have an amazingly long reach. NASA believes it has managed to mark the distant edge of the President's ego.

And, perhaps most amazing, the Hubble has discovered many inhabited worlds! NASA teams knew they were on the brink of such discoveries when a road sign was revealed, 400 light years away, that read, "You have now reached the Gated Suburban Connecticut Galaxy. Please keep driving."

The Hubble found a fascinating planet with two Suns, a world where all decisions were made based on a monstrous government manual, issued by the Department of Redundancy Department. On this planet, citizens spend most of their lives standing in the wrong line, fuming, because they had been given the wrong form in the previous line, which was in an alternate dimension, in a building that no longer exists.

The US Congress quickly put together a fact-finding junket, eager to learn some new tricks. Sadly, though, the exploration team ran out of food while waiting for an entry visa, and had to secure a loan from ACORN's "prostitution and family planning" division.

The Hubble discovered a planet where people had post-existing conditions. Imagine! They had conditions that they didn't even have yet. And we think it's hard getting health insurance coverage *here*.

The telescope located one planet where a government official, an all-growed-up human being, makes the claim that house pets should be able to sue their owners.

No it didn't. The Hubble did not locate any such thing. There's no such planet in the universe. No species is that stupid.

But it did find a planet populated by 5 billion beings - and every single one of them was a *unique* species.

Yep. A planet comprised of 100% minorities.

The White House, noting this new bloc of potential voters, whipped up plans for an intergalactic speech, but couldn't work out the logistics for setting up synched teleprompters in two different galaxies.

And the universe smiled.

Jarping with Ostara

(An American tale of children, mutant rabbits, and flak jackets)

Looking for ways to add some spice to your next Easter Egg Hunt? Here's an idea: call in an air strike.

Not long ago, my church held its annual Easter Egg Hunt, and I had a chance to volunteer my valuable services, which begin with my uncanny ability to recognize an egg, and end with my unmatched talent of being able to spot an entirely different egg. Obviously, my church family welcomed my participation; after all, cognitive skills of such scope generally don't come cheap.

That morning, as I arrived, I noticed a couple of nondescript guys taking good advantage of the broad, clear field that separates the church from the facing road. The pair were spending their Saturday morning flying a remote-control fighter jet up and over and around the field. "This works," I reasoned. "How better to add that just-right touch of missing mania than to combine candy-crazed children with an atavistic pagan ritual and the potential threat of being randomly strafed by enemy fire?"

But, ultimately, the ever-eager local news stations were denied. The closest we came to actual physical danger occurred while the designated grown-ups were hiding the eggs, when someone discovered an undiscovered egg from LAST year and nearly ate the rancid foil-covered chocolate hidden within. Not exactly a Homeland Security color-code switcher, but it did provide a moment of tension.

How, do you suppose, did our country come to embrace this seasonal tradition? Where did this unlikely egg-laying Easter Bunny come from? What does this fertile little chocolate-pushing Peep pimp have to do with Easter? And most importantly: somewhere, there's a company that makes all that fake plastic grass we shove inside the Easter baskets. What do they do the rest of the year?

History tells us that Christopher Columbus did not, in fact, discover the Easter Bunny, because George Bush unfairly quarantined the poor little animal at Gitmo during the infamous Cheney Purges that followed a vile, government-conspiracy-backed attack on New York City real estate during th...

Oh, wait. Sorry. That's what *revisionist* history tells us. I'll begin again.

History tells us that many cultures have worshiped, or at least honored, or at least respected, or at least eaten, eggs. An ancient Latin phrase, *Omne vivum ex ovo*, makes the claim that "all life comes from an egg," a maxim attributed to an oft-quoted Roman Prostate, Foghornus Leghornus. This, however, cannot be confirmed, since the Prostate was ambushed in the year MCHAMMR by a myopic midget, Elmer Fuddus, during the Ides of Sweeps Week.

But the legend may precede Rome. According to my research, conducted in-between hourly emails teasing me to switch car insurance companies, the ancient Persians painted eggs for Nowrooz, their celebration of the New Year, which for the Persians began on the Spring Aquanauts, probably because nobody could spell "January."

Later, during medieval times (literal translation: "oh, about 50% evil"), people were forbidden to eat eggs during Lent, but nobody told the medieval chickens. So every year, as the Lenten season approached, tradition called for households to hurry up and eat all their on-hand eggs, and this logically led to another tradition known as Pancake Day. Well, of course it did.

At one point in time, people believed that eggs laid on Good Friday were particularly special. If you held on to these special eggs for 100 years, legend predicted that two things would happen:

1) The egg yolks would turn to solid gold
2) You would be dead

The Anglo-Saxons had a noted fondness for Eastre, the goddess of Spring. To other groups, she was variously known as Eostre, The Egg Babe, Peep Woman, and

Jennifer Anniston. The Germans called her Ostara, a name simply dreamed up by that rascal, story-teller Jakob Grimm, whose brother Ben went on to become an entirely fictional character, and helped found the Fantastic Four.

In northern England, a traditional Easter-time game has players hitting each other's hard-boiled eggs. Apparently, the citizenry get quite excited about this group activity, and if you've ever watched cricket, you can sympathize. The traditional game is known, for obvious reasons, as "egg jarping." Well, of course it is.

A very similar game is a crowd pleaser in the Republic of Srpska (pronounced "Cleveland"), but for obvious, logical reasons, they call it "tucanje" (literal translation: "celebrity vampire bowling"). Well, of cpzet they ꞔdahj.

Oddly enough, a very similar game is played in southern Louisiana, where the locals refer to the activity as "Pocking Eggs," and if I started right now, and lived till my yolks gilded, I'd still be coming up with impolite jokes for that one.

One more historical note: I'm told that the Passover Seder rituals include dipping a hard-boiled egg in salt water, which symbolizes new life, and totally rules out any hope of anyone getting a nice omelet.

But that's their business. My job is to observe, not to judge.

Meanwhile, back here at home: our egg hunt went well...for a while. We had scheduled a first round of egg-hunting, then a little diversionary craft-making time while the grown-ups collected and re-hid the eggs, then a second round. We managed to hide all the eggs for the first round, and the church grounds were absolutely dripping with festive little plastic eggs, red and pink, green and yellow, striped and polka-dotted, and even a few that had been painted like guerilla military camouflage (I'm guessing it was a male grown-up who dreamed that up).

As a witness to the egg-hunting contest, I learned something, too. Unlike grown-ups, children, when asked to declare how many eggs they found, will just tell you the truth. No greed, no guile, no raging ego. Just...the truth.

How refreshing.

But then, before the second round, signals somehow got mixed. Suddenly, sugar-saturated kids erupted from the building for "Egg Hunt: The Sequel" before we had finished hiding all the eggs. So I just started lobbing eggs out of my little Egg Master bag, randomly jarping them at incoming children, occasionally checking the sky for incoming artillery. Soon, I had this odd, Pied Piper-like, tailing appendage of small humans. Three of them followed me home.

So now I have three new, cute, little chocolate-stained tax deductions, and free lawn care.

And I'm glad they're here. I'll need their help to keep an eye on these rogue guerilla eggs.

Otis, Isis and the Evil Empire

(Dracula. Health insurance. Solar flares. Egypt. All connected. Who knew?)

Last week was tough. Not only was there the looming threat of Earth being bombarded by massive solar storms; I also had to negotiate with my health insurance provider, Evil Inc.

It would've been easier to argue with the storms.

According to scientists, intense solar storms are slinging plasma bombs toward Earth, which could seriously disrupt global communications. According to doctors, for years I've been playing host to a half-dozen unnecessary, uninvited, undocumented residents known as diverticula, which sounds like one of the vampires I met on Facebook.

And according to Evil Inc., my chances of receiving any diverticula-based medical reimbursements are about the same as my chances of being hit on the left arm, in a Bangkok side-street at exactly 8:27 PM, by a solar plasma bomb named Alfred.

Day to day, medically-speaking, diverticula just kind of sit there, like tenured teachers. This is a medical condition known as Diverticula-Otis. But there's just not a whole lot going on, entertainment-wise, in your average colon (many rural colons don't even have high-speed internet). So sometimes, out of boredom, or just plain meanness, the Diverticula Posse will get infected, a condition known as Diverticula-Isis. (This is not to be confused with Diverticula-Osiris, which is a form of gum disease found in ancient Egyptian winged insects, from which we get the term "plaque of locusts.")

LITERARY SIDEBAR: Diverticula is the plural of universticula, which means "one verticula." Verticula is an ancient Egyptian term that means "over-priced window treatments." It's the opposite of Horizonticula, which means "window treatments installed by my wife's idiot nephew."

So, you see, my problem is two-fold. Since my diverticula are already here, Evil Inc. considers my situation a "pre-existing condition," which is evil-health-insurance-company-speak for "not covered by your policy." But since the diverticula are, to use a highly technical medical term, "inside me," it requires a screening procedure to see if they're up to any truant behavior. And Evil Inc. insists that a "screening procedure" is "not covered by your policy."

Now if your diverticula ever do go rogue and get infected, then you need to do one of two things, depending on your health insurance provider: seek immediate medical attention, or get struck by a solar plasma bomb. Getting struck by a solar plasma bomb is known as a "non-existing condition." (Oddly enough, Evil Inc. will cover *that*.)

PHILOSOPHICAL SIDEBAR: Isn't ***every*** condition a pre-existing condition? How can you have a ***post***-existing condition? If a condition isn't pre-existing, well, you don't have it yet.

Maybe that's the marketing plan at Evil Inc. We'll cover anything you don't have. If you get what you don't have, get out. From then on, you're on your own.

And to further complicate my insurance issues, my doctor recommends I submit to this preventive, potentially life-saving screening procedure, called a "colonoscopy," simply because I've reached the age of 50. Imagine! As if my ***doctor*** should have anything to say about my medical condition. Absurd. That's why we have a government.

POLITICAL SIDEBAR: Health insurance is, admittedly, quite complicated. But there's only one entity in this galaxy that could possibly manage to make things worse ... and they're working on it as we speak. One day soon, if you have a sore throat, you'll have to go to the Post Office, submit to a full thoracic exam and knee-jerk-reaction test, pick up some thirty-dollar stamps, wait in line for six months, and you'll come home with a carbon credit, somebody else's throat, and a Government Motors truck muffler bolted to your neck.

The stamps, by the way, will have a picture of a Muslim Elvis. And by the time you get home, they'll be useless, due to a postal rate hike.

I've now talked to Evil Inc. five times about the upcoming screening procedure, and I've gotten five different answers. As far as I can follow their evil-policy-speak, it looks like they'll cover part of the cost of either the doctor's boat payment, or three band-aids, whichever is determined to be least helpful to me, but only if the procedure is performed on a Wednesday, at a table (not a booth) in a Starbucks, in the presence of a left-handed Anglican elder who has less than three bipedal children currently attending a liberal arts college, unless the college offers classes, or has a lawn.

Witness:

INC: "Thanks for calling Evil Inc. Your call is very important to us, although you're gonna find that awfully hard to believe as you spend the next 2 or 3 hours navigating our Customer Service phone queue, a brilliantly complex maze that was rejected by the IRS as being too complicated. For quality and training purposes, your call may be monitored. For legal and statistical purposes, your call may be answered. To continue in English, press or say Xochiquetzal."

[time]

Me: "Evil customer service representative, I have a question about my coverage."

INC: "Your *WHAT?*"

Me: "I have a standard medical procedure scheduled, designed to detect any problems early. Is that covered?"

INC: "HA! Good one! *[Hey, Ed, pick up! Listen to THIS guy! Whoo!]*"

LEGAL SIDEBAR: My insurance company isn't really named Evil Inc. I won't share their actual name, because they have, to use a highly technical medical term, "lawyers out the kazoo." But I can tell you that their name can be rearranged to spell "Harsh Sultanate." Also, "Anal Haste Hurts."

Coincidence? I think not.

INC: "Thanks for calling Evil Inc. How can I ignore you?"

Me: "I'd like to buy some health insurance."

INC: "No problem. We'll insure your health all day long. It's that "lack of health" condition that gets tricky."

Me: "What if I get sick?"

INC: "Please hold."

[time]

INC: "You're still holding?"

Me: "Yeah."

INC: "Weird. Nobody's ever done *that* before."

Me: "Forget the health insurance. I'd like to buy some life insurance."

INC: "I'm sorry, sir or madam. Life is a pre-existing condition."

Me: "Yeah, okay. Fair enough. But one day, I'll be dead."

INC: "Hold on, sir or madam, I'll transfer you to Eschatology."

RELIGIOUS SIDEBAR: For those of you who missed the annual "Theology Day" at public school, or had a tenured teacher, eschatology is the study of Eschatol, an ancient Egyptian deity who was in charge of Red Sea crowd control, and intestinal disorders brought on by eating too many really spicy lamb sandwiches.

INC: "This is Evil Inc. calling. Am I speaking to valued customer Mrs. Bart Parknet?"

Me: [sigh] "Sure. Go ahead."

INC: "This is Screwtape, from the Eschatology department. We're not gonna be able to cover your life, Mr. Partknot. You need to die before your policy renewal date. Will that be a problem? We can defer your premium, Mrs. Barkledge, if that's more convenient. After all, our focus is all about you, Burl. Can I call you Burl?"

FOXNEWS ALERT: Plasma bombs, lobbed from the sun's surface by former US President George Bush, have further delayed BP's efforts to stop the Gulf oil spill, and now threaten to disrupt global communications, particularly in rural colons. However, a White House spokesman claims that all is well, noting that President Obama has donned a cape and is flying towards the sun.

INC: "Thanks for calling Evil Inc. My name is Wormwood. How can we take your money?"

Undocumented Worker: "I'm a lawn guy that works for one of your customers. I think he's dead."

INC: "Whatever. Why are you calling *us?*"

UW: "I don't know the number for 9-1-1. Hey, he looks pretty dead."

INC: "Not our problem. Technically, death is not a medical condition. But just for the benefit of our Christmas party ... how can you tell he's dead?"

UW: "I put on an Ella Fitzgerald album. Not a twitch. No hay movimiento alguno."

INC: "Hey! Are you an illegal alien?"

UW: "Uh, I, um. Could be."

INC: "Well, *you* we can cover!"

MEDICAL SIDEBAR: For those of you who are wondering what we'll be discussing next week, a colonoscopy is a medical procedure designed to introduce middle-aged people to new vocabulary words, like "terminal ileum" and "sigmoid" and "wallet extraction."

INC: "This is Evil Inc. calling. Am I speaking to valued customer Barley Parsons?"

Me: [sigh] "Yeah."

INC: "Mr. Parlay, since you didn't die, we just wanted to remind you of our customer referral program!"

Me: "Holy Eschatol. You have *got* to be kidding me."

INC: "Kidding? No, Mrs. Parcels. As a requirement for employment at Evil Inc., I had my sense of humor surgically removed."

Me: "Huh. How much does *that* cost?"

INC: "Sorry, Mr. Pardol, your medical policy doesn't cover medical procedures. Would you like to purchase an upgrade?"

Me: "*UPGRADE?* WHY DON'T YOU UPGRADE *THIS,* YOU MISERABLE SACK O..."

[Communication interrupted by solar plasma bombs]

Duke Sigmoid's Vuvuzela

(The 'aging' dance continues. And I thought *eyebrow dandruff* was bad.)

First of all, let's give credit where due. I tip my hat to my hero, Dave Barry, who beat me to this topic. As a result of his groundbreaking medical research, Dave has made it harder for a humorist to *write about* a colonoscopy than to actually *have* a colonoscopy.

Thanks a lot, Dave.

A Brief History of Invasive Surgery

Recently, I was a more-or-less unwilling participant in an age-based rite of passage that goes something like this: "Oh, you're fifty years old? Well, let's get you naked, define the most unlikely spot imaginable and then insert a camera!"

First off, I had no idea I was fifty. I haven't seen my wrist-watch since college, when an old roommate "borrowed" it so he wouldn't "stay up too late" at a "friendly poker game." Of course, I never "saw him again."

Now to be fair, a colonoscopy is a fairly common procedure these days, if you define "fairly common" as being starved, purged, drugged, prodded, and having several total strangers co-star with some of your internal organs in a reality show that you can't watch, but which you get to pay for.

What this entire endoscopic exercise does is this: it gives you a whole new appreciation for the term "private sector." Hopefully, this is as close to prison as I'll ever get.

After resigning to my fate, my first chore was to go to the hospital and have some blood drawn. For reasons that were never explained, my potassium levels were critical. Maybe the film crew were worried that the camera's light would break, and the doctors would have to strike a match.

Lawyers, who are trained to spot anyone facing this pending procedure by that "hunted duck" look in the patient's eyes, surrounded me in the hospital lobby, loading me up with business cards and oversized refrigerator magnets.

The sign-in counter at the hospital's lab featured all the standard forms. You know: sign in; write your name; your birthday; your doctor's name; the time you arrived; no, the time you *really* arrived; now be honest - we were watching the clock when you arrived; your gender; the gender you would like to be if you worked for the city of San Francisco; why you think your medical condition is George Bush's fault; have you ever been bitten in the afflicted area by a ferret, and so on. Standard stuff.

But on *this* counter was another form: some kind of internal Employee Recognition project, obviously printed in-house, bearing this bold-cap title: "THEY KEY TO THEIR SUCCESS IS YOU!"

Not a very good feeling, knowing you're putting your life in the hands of a gang that can't spell "the."

Insurance, we already discussed, elsewhere. Since I was well, it didn't go well. My health insurance non-provider (Evil Inc.) indignantly refused to discuss paying for stuff that happened before I got sick, or that didn't involve me currently being sick, or screening procedures or anything else that might possibly keep me from getting sick. On the plus side, though, should I ever get sick, they promised to show me how a simple screening procedure could have prevented my getting sick, just before they promised to refuse to pay for anything I needed until before or after I was no longer not sick.

Here's how bad Evil Inc. is: even President Obama can't help. It's true! I called him, personally, on his Bat Phone. Eight times. Each time, he was on another vacation.

The Ever-Popular Cleansing Day

On this topic, there's just not much left to say that hasn't already been said. Let's go with an allegory.

In a nutshell, you've got a colon for sale. Tomorrow morning, your realtor, a member of the Million Dollar

Colon Roundtable Club, is coming by with a "hot" buyer in tow. The eager buyer is Duke Sigmoid and his life partner, the Duchess of Ileum, who lost their own colon due to a glitch in the Universal Health Care Bill. Your colon, like your college dorm room, hasn't seen a broom or a mop since the Truman Administration. There are actual pizza stains on the ceiling fan in the great room (what doctors call the "intestium crassum," if they're doctors with a really good sense of humor).

And now you've got exactly one day to make the place spotless.

Fear not. Extremely bitter people have invented drugs that will do to you exactly what you need to have done to you, which is, coincidentally, exactly what needs to be done to Congress.

How does the cleansing process work? Let's whip out another allegory. Imagine yourself as the cleansing drug. You walk into a long, narrow room, filled with old college roommates who owe you money and a wristwatch. A violent chemical reaction occurs. Boom. Room empty.

Got it?

The Day Time Stood Still

Pre-op was mostly just a case of self-inflicted nerves; you know, the way anybody would feel when people are about to play "Up Periscope" and you've been tagged as

The Surface Of The Ocean. The hospital staff was just as kind and helpful as they could be, but they kept dancing by, hitting me with statements one doesn't normally hear in an average workday.

- "Hi, I'm Mindy. I'll be sticking a needle in your wrist!"
- "Hi, I'm Teencie. I'll be putting all your clothes and your wallet in a large un-tagged plastic bag."
- "Hi, I'm a patient in the bed partition beside yours. Have you any Grey Poupon?"
- "Hi, I'm Detective Phillips. We're looking for a troublemaker named Norwood. Domestic violence case. Keep your eyes open. Here's my card."
- "Hi, I'm new here. Are post-op patients always that bruised?"
- "Hi, I'm a large, unshaven man. I'll be waiting behind this curtain until you take off all your clothes."
- "Hi, I'm an imaginary character in a bad dream you're having. Wow. You sure do bruise easily!"
- "Hi, I'm Norwood. I'll be in charge of administering drugs through that needle in your wrist until you're irretrievably unconscious, and then later, if all goes well - and if my infuriating ex-wife and her grope-crazed attorney will leave me ALONE FOR FIVE BLOODY SECONDS - I'll be bringing you back to life."

In the bed partition next to me were 3 female members of the Tank Top Nation, Momma and 2 daughters, estimated combined tonnage: 750 lbs (excluding tattoos). Momma wasn't happy to be "kep waden" for something that "weren't my [bleep] idear na furz [bleepin'] place." She spent the morning calling people on her daughter's "sale foam," threatening to tell "at dock" that he could kiss a specific, albeit broad, segment of her south-facing tonnage.

My, that woman could swear.

High Noon

Truth be told, I remember more about my Senior Prom.

I was wheeled in to the O.R. and coddled like someone who, if treated very nicely, could be convinced to disclose the location of a bunch of hidden money. Then I was coaxed to roll over onto my left side. That's when I noticed the high-def camera suspended from the ceiling. In the screen, I could see my partial contour, lying on my side, and several serious figures in the background, purposefully scurrying back and forth among complicated pieces of machinery. I felt like I was in an episode of '24.'

Shortly, Mindy (or it could have been Teencie, or Detective Phillips) leaned in and said, "Okay, I'm gonna put you under. Ready?"

"Okay," I said. "But I still think we should see other people."

Next, the surgeon walked in, wearing a mask, and said, "Gimme all your money!"

I'm kidding. That didn't happen till later.

And then, as Hunter Thompson might put it, the drugs kicked in.

After the Dance (the post-op)

"Barry?"

I snapped awake. And a good thing, too, because I'd been deep in the grip of an anesthesia-induced nightmare involving androgynous nurses from San Francisco who kept urging me not to vote for Proposition 8.

It was done! I asked a few "how'd it go" questions, but I quickly shut up. We tend to forget that these Operating Room people are paid professionals, who do this all the time. And because they do this all the time, they get bored.

Remember the World Cup games in South Africa, and that constant, hypnotic, never-ending one-note blare from the crowd? That multi-hour single-tone symphony was generated by hundreds of three-foot-long Zulu horns, known as *vuvuzela*. Now, I'm not saying that my O.R. crew had access to a vuvuzela. But they do get bored.

And when I came to, *my hair was parted on the other side.*

But, at least it was over. Well, almost. Thanks to Evil Inc. and *their* single-tone symphony (*no no no no no no no no no*), we had one more procedure to complete. So I leaned over one more time, and the nice doctor deftly performed a full wallet extraction.

The First Day of the Rest of My Life

Afterwards, once I got home, I had a sore throat. I don't want to think about that.

And I did get photos, though they're not exactly the sort of wallet-sized proof-sheet winners that you whip out at the office water cooler.

"Hey, Fred! Looka my sigmoid!"

"Congratulations. Looks just like you, Harold."

But it wasn't a total loss. One photo clearly shows Geraldo Rivera closing in on Jimmy Hoffa.

Most importantly, I'm home. Home from my visit with the local hospital's Rear Admiral, with a clean bill of health, along with several other extremely clean things. Home, and healthy. Nice feeling, that. And I didn't nick a single one of Dave Barry's jokes.

Oh, and they found my watch.

Godzilla Gets A Praline

(How music saved America from several scary monsters)

Day 2,241 of the Gulf Oil Spill. The third tactical nuke has failed to garrote the gusher.

And in the French Quarter, Godzilla is still at large.

Meanwhile, all along America's southern coast, nature is busily maladjusting. Entire ecosystems have packed and punted. Well-represented oysters won their class-action lawsuit, mass-migrated upriver to Memphis, and opened a wildly popular blues club called "Salt-Tune Crackers." Pensacola realtors are raking it in, having capitalized on some clever rezoning after the city was renamed "La Brea Phase II." Louisiana is a science experiment, Mobile went mobile, and Key West is a petro Petri dish. Nations of shrimp gave up the Gulf Coast ghost, chipped in on a moving van, and relocated to a spare bedroom in Pat Conroy's house.

The mounting public pressure seems to be getting the best of BP. Today, an unnamed spokesman testily commented that "Louisiana ain't the only place to get shrimp." Vice President Joe Biden called BP's comment a "big (expletive) deal" and then leaked the name of the spokesman, along with the location of several strategic oil reserves and our nuclear launch codes. Biden's facts were challenged by press veteran Helen Thomas who, as a cub reporter, covered the creation of oil during the Jurassic.

JAZZ UPDATE: Godzilla shows up with a trap set and sits in on a hot jam session at Preservation Hall. Gape-jawed music fans can't get enough of his funky "one-and-three shuffle."

Concerning the oil spill, White House spokesman Robert "Obviously" Gibbs insists that the current administration is "really close" to having a plan. When pressed by a reporter for details, Gibbs said he refuses to discuss hypotheticals. Sadly, Gibbs was then pecked to death by several exhausted-looking mammals, including brown pelicans and Helen Thomas.

Following BP's latest failed solution (the "Rope-A-Dope"), anxious Americans awaited news of their latest effort (the "Shut Up & Sing"). Apparently, this scheme involves having the oil geyser attend an eight-week Planet Sensitivity Training seminar, co-chaired by soft-spoken guru, Deep-pocket Chopra, and his wife, Oprah Chopra. The hope is that the bubbling crude will become wracked with guilt and surrender to China, so that China can then sell our own fuel right back to us in America.

JAZZ UPDATE: Godzilla waddled in to the Satchmo Summerfest with a trumpet, a Hotty Toddy hat, and a serious mojo. His soulful rendition of "Can't We Be Friends" leaves several attending patrons in need of oxygen.

As we know, all of BP's earlier plans were miserable failures, despite their high-tech tactics (mud), their radical alternatives (druid chants), and their public relations miscues ("Hey, you've still got 46 other states"). Their now-infamous "voodoo child" project, that involved sacrificing a live chicken in a graveyard at midnight, went horribly wrong. As a result, scores of horrid, muttering, wild-eyed creatures were unleashed, including undead zombies and Helen Thomas.

And that's when the White House called on Hollywood.

We ought to have seen that one coming. Given that we have a President whose entire leadership resume consists of reading his lines from a prompter while standing in front of fake Greek columns, pulling in Hollywood talent was only a matter of time.

Hollywood director James "Titanic" Cameron was the obvious choice to save our entire hemisphere, because he once used underwater cameras. Earlier today, Cameron (now Secretary of the Interior) held his daily briefing with Quentin "Reservoir Dogs" Tarantino (now head of FEMA) and the newly-appointed Special Effects Czar, Steven Spielberg (director of "Helen Thomas: The Extra-Terrestrial"). President Obama, who was still vacationing at a Chicago part-the-water park, restated his opinion that things should be what he thinks things should be, when things are not the things he thinks things are.

JAZZ UPDATE: On closing night at the Voodoo, Godzilla stomped on-stage during The Subdudes' set, whipped out a jaw-harp, and dedicated "All The Time In The World" to Helen Thomas. Observers say that several members of the audience were so overcome with emotion at Godzilla's interpretation that they converted to Shinto.

After Secretary Cameron reviewed the failures of BP's earlier attempts (the top hat, top kill, hat kill, side kill, just-a-bit-off-to-the-side kill and road kill), he admitted to seeing some promise in a Tarantino idea ("Kill Bill"). Unfortunately, Cameron's plot went awry when a robotic saw blade from the future went rogue, clawing its way through the floor of the Gulf. Deep, dark places were exposed, and things were disturbed that should not have been disturbed, including Godzilla and Helen Thomas.

And the rest is history.

NEWS UPDATE: This just in. Godzilla's live album, a Miles Davis tribute titled "Kind of Green," has been nominated for a Grammy. The album is a sales rocket at amazon.com, and Godzilla has been tagged as King of the Crewe for the next Mardi Gras.

And a DNA scan has confirmed that Helen Thomas is actually a Muppet.

Worldshaker

(History: it's all about big guns and bad beer.)

It's done. The jury is in. Weird has a new world champion.

Until recently, the most bizarre people I had ever met were some beer-fueled fraternity guys in Athens, Georgia. Apparently, this crew were pursuing a Bachelor's Degree in disturbing the peace, with a minor in falling off balconies. These guys put the "dys" in "dysfunctional."

But that was before I met Pachakuti. Hang up the phone, folks: we have a winner.

In the 1400s, a very focused social climber in Peru changed history, and created a whole bunch of potential jokes. His name was Wiraqocha which, as far as we know, was not his fault. Wiraqocha became known as the first Inka (literal translation: "I have more soldiers than you"). He changed his name to Wiraqocha Inka (this was entirely his fault) and settled his family in Qosqo (literal translation: "Costco").

Historical Sidebar: The Spanish referred to Qosqo as "Cusco," which is a strong indictment against Spain's public education system.

Things went well for about 8 minutes, until King Wiraqocha's clan was attacked by the fierce Chanka (literal translation: "fraternity guys"). The valiant Inka King yelled something about conquering "half the world," then shoved his family into the Qoztetzlmizkotl (literal translation:"SUV") and valiantly ran away.

But not the whole family. A younger son (Inka Cusi Yupanki) stayed in Costco, defeated the Chanka, and then, as part of an unorthodox fraternity hazing ritual, skinned them.

Historical Sidebar: The Spanish referred to the Inka as "savages," leading anthropologists to posit that Spain, at least once during the 15th Century, must have visited Athens, Georgia.

King Wiraqocha was well-pleased with his younger son, Yupanki, and to show his gratitude, plotted to have the youngster killed. But Yupanki, like many young people today, didn't know how to accept a gift graciously. Yupanki rebelled against his father, the King valiantly ran away again, and Yupanki took over management of Costco, renaming himself Pachakuti (literal translation: "Worldshaker").

Quickly, the Worldshaker got busy, running up and down the Andes, conquering everything in sight. For 25 years, he participated in an early form of political redistricting that spread savagery and wild decadence from Costco to Lake Titicaca and, ultimately, to Athens, Georgia.

Administration of the expanding empire fell to the Worldshaker's son, Thupa Inka Yupanki (literal translation: "Rahm Emanuel"). Thupa, lacking the grandiose ambition of his father, the Worldshaker, gave himself the princely ceremonial name Tsodium Qloride Kuti ("Saltshaker").

As Pachakuti's influence grew, so did his greed (much like the United States in our time). He named his empire Tawantinsuyu (literal translation: "anagram for 'Tuna was Unity'") and built the magnificent, gold-plated central plaza of Awkaypata (anagram: "Paw at a Yak"), which became known as the crown of Mother Earth, or "Pacha Mama" (see "whole bunch of potential jokes").

And, much like the United States in our time, the whole scheme ran on no money whatsoever.

In 1471, Pachakuti died peacefully, or not. Suddenly, Thupa the Saltshaker was King, and it went straight to his little Inka head. Thupa declared himself a god (literal translation: "member of Congress") and insisted on being hauled around in a golden litter. As he was carted up and down the aisles of Costco, lying in his litter, the awed citizenry would get so carried away by his glory that they would pull out their eyebrows and eyelashes, and that's where we get the expression "bald-faced lie."

Historical Sidebar: Thupa thought the ground was not worthy of receiving his holy saliva, so when he had the need, Thupa would simply spit in the hand of a nearby courtier, and that's where we get the expression "TGIF."

Thupa began the custom of marrying one's own sister, a custom that's still practiced in some of the more hilly regions of the United States. In fact, according to some historians, he married two of his sisters. And these were in addition to his two or three hundred subordinate wives. And that's where we get the expression "masochistic moron."

In 1493, Thupa died, possibly due to extreme conjugal exhaustion, or an overdose of nagging. This time, succession was bound to get tricky, since Ole Salty had fathered over sixty sons. So the "negotiations" began, resulting in (surprise!) the oldest heir getting killed. The surviving son took the name Wayna Qhapaq ("Wayne Newton") and became The Inka, though he wasn't yet old enough to act like a true idiot. Until he came of age, two uncles ran the Costco, until (surprise!) one uncle killed the other. Once Wayne Newton reached his majority, he (surprise!) killed two of his brothers and (surprise!) married his sister.

Wayne's son, Atawallpa ("Wal-Mart Inka"), looked greedily to the east and took a stab at annexing Ecuador, but the natives there apparently weren't interested in incest. Nevertheless, the Inka armies prevailed, after which Wayne settled into some kind of depressed funk. Historians tell us that for the next 6 years, King Wayne just moped around in Ecuador, wearing a vampire-bat wool shirt and getting drunk on chicha, a muddy, maize-based beer commonly found in Athens, Georgia. As you might imagine, this dark era was peppered with massive resignations by scores of saliva catchers, who ultimately unionized (United Phlegm

Workers Local 23) and struck for better wages, just before they were all (surprise!) killed.

In 1525, at the end of this era (literal translation: "will this be on the test?"), Wayne died after falling off a fraternity balcony. Following the inevitable non-bloodless intrigue, one of Wayne's teenage sons won the day and named himself Washkar Inka (literal translation: "The God of Drive-Thru Auto Cleaning"). The sulking, overlooked Atawallpa stayed in Ecuador and opened a chicha microbrewery. King Washkar took Dad's body back home, killed everybody within 6 degrees of separation, and then (surprise!) married his sister.

Historical Sidebar: Shortly after returning home, King Washkar found out that his mom (his dad's sister) had not actually, technically, married his dad, so he forced her to have a dart-gun wedding ceremony with Dad's mummy. As one historian drily put it, "even for the Andes this was an unusual step."

Washkar and Atawallpa spent the next few years trying to sneak up on each other with a sharpened llama bone. Legally, Atawallpa's claims to the throne were a bit weak, since *his* mom was only his father's cousin. The shame! I mean, how nearly not undisgraceful is *that*?

After 3 years, Atawallpa was captured and imprisoned, but his wife (named "Aunt Doris") snuck an atavistic proto-crowbar into the prison, and he managed to escape by digging his way out. Insulted, under-medicated and armed with an atavistic proto-crowbar, Atawallpa quickly captured Washkar's head general ("Uncle Doris"), cut off the general's head, stuck a bowl on it, filled it with chicha, and shared a drink with his own generals. And that's where we get the expression "beer head," not to mention "yuck."

Atawallpa and his army then headed back to Costco for the final smackdown. Washkar Inka was captured and forced to marry himself. Atawallpa, the newest Inka, started interviewing sisters.

And then, as so often happens in history, one of those bizarre coincidences occurred, a credibility-testing coincidence, like the Pilgrims sailing from a place called Plymouth, England, and then just happening to land in America at a place called Plymouth Rock.

As Atawallpa Inka was busily setting up his government and selecting Saliva Boys, a courier arrived from the coast, breathlessly informing the new King that tall ships had landed, carrying pale hairy men who sat atop enormous animals.

Yes. It was Siegfried and Roy.

Historical Sidebar: No, it wasn't.

It was Francisco Pizarro, the conquistador (literal translation: "insecure male manifesting over-compensation issues during a mid-life crisis"). The Spanish had arrived. The ultimate undocumented workers had breached the border. And as quickly as the empire of the Inka had risen, it fell even more quickly.

The Inka had slings. The Spanish had horses and armor, guns and cannon. The Inka had rooms full of gold and silver. The Spanish had, well, horses and armor, guns and cannon. It was pretty much over by lunch.

Pizarro and 168 men had just taken down the greatest empire on earth.

And that, students, is where we get the expression "Second Amendment."

Actuarial Family Theater

(Risk management, food chains, neurotic rabbits, and evil sea aliens)

I'm a single guy. But I do have married friends. And some of those friends have children. And this week, I waded across that border, into a birthday party for the daughter of a couple I know. A lovely couple they are, with two lovely children named Tierney and Kit, several pets, a high deductible, and nerves of hammered steel.

I had no idea.

Amazingly, nobody died. By evening's end I was utterly shell-shocked, but I slinked away, unharmed, re-armed with some critical intelligence:

1. I'm not ready for a family.
2. On Planet Children, different rules apply. One plus one does not equal two. The energy envelope generated by two children is affected by some kind of mystical energy multiplier.
3. You simply cannot trust magic sea-monkeys.

Living alone, I'm used to a state of quiet. In my house, there are almost never any altercations involving fauna eating other fauna. I seldom invest in bags of what look like dirt particles, expecting them to magically morph into underwater primates. Sugar ingestion rarely results in psychotic behavior, undersized humans don't don TRON outfits and wheels to break indoor speed limits, and I can't even recall the last food fight. As someone clever once said, "If something gets broke, I know who broke it." True, there are weekend poker games that sometimes present some unexpected surprises, but I own a broom and a gun. Problem solved.

When viewed with Single Guy eyes, a home with kids and pets in it is a black-diamond slope, navigated in the dark. An extreme theme park ride, sans seat belts. A Marx Brothers finale, but with live ammo.

As someone clever once said, "Same planet, different worlds."

Witness:

I drove to my friends' place, parked, ran through sheets of rain to the front door, and rang the doorbell. A large, moist dog materialized out of some alternate dimension and attempted to smell areas of me that I don't generally present for public inspection.

After the dog and I agreed to an annulment, I tuned to a growing rumble inside the house. One of the children answered the door. He was wearing pajamas, a helmet, knee- and elbow-pads, and inline roller skates. He looked like a psychotic Munchkin.

"Is that for me?"
"No, Kit, this is Tierney's birthday present."
"Mmm."

Kit reversed and rolled away. I stepped into the hall and tripped over a real rabbit.

In my house, I almost never collide with small forest animals.

The damp dog shot through the door, brushed me aside and, in a tender protective gesture, attempted to hide the whole rabbit in its mouth.

"KIT!" a voice boomed from the kitchen. "THE DOG!"

Kit glared at me with that "wonder if he'll leave soon" look, grabbed the dog, wrenched it back outside, and shut the door.

Over the next few hours, I learned a great deal about kids, pets, and perpetual motion. I learned that food fights can get really interesting when the ordnance is birthday cake squares, with the candles still lit. I learned that an entrepreneur could pull down some serious coin by opening a McRabbit restaurant for dogs.

I learned that parents have an acutely-attuned sense of hearing. At various points during the evening, we would all hear thuds, howls, and other oral effects straight out of the Spanish Inquisition. Sometimes the parents would leap into action, sometimes not.

In my house, one blood-curdling shriek sounds pretty much like any other.

Eventually, Tierney completed her excavation of Gift Mountain, unearthing her own pair of inline roller skates, assorted books, clothing, jewelry, some fish, an arcane-looking Magic Sea-Monkeys Castle kit, and another live rabbit. The dog, observing from outside, grinned at the new rabbit, mouthed "make your peace, lunch-meat" and then went back to picking the lock.

I spent the rest of the evening edgily watching kids on wheels race from room to room, caroming off countertops and other sharp objects. Every few seconds I would instinctively leap up to steady a skewing skater, or to dodge a dog, or to extract a rabbit. Occasionally, I'd hear faint chanting, and thick green smoke would boil out of the sea-monkeys' magic castle.

After a time, the kids deserted the house to skate outside. In their pajamas. In the dark. In the rain. And, no doubt, armed with scissors and cake-square firebombs.

Some 87 lifetimes later, the cavalry finally arrived. Bedtime.

"Tierney! Kit!"

I shot out of my chair to find and retrieve a towel, but suddenly my Single Guy ears adjusted. "Oh. Sorry. I thought you yelled 'tourniquet.'"

And parents do this every day.

I had no idea. Before crossing the border, I should have sent in drones. I should have acquired better intelligence. As someone clever once said, "When you're in enemy territory, never get out of the boat."

Especially when there are sea-monkeys.

Me Two Gets Her Way

(Odd bedfellows collide in one of America's possible futures)

My clone and I were driving the kids over to Gitmo North for sensitivity training when the rogue Toyota toaster oven lurched into the skyway.

My clone, Me Two, blamed me. I was using Robo-Steer, of course - I'm not a total idiot - and it's not as if I had *asked* the toaster oven to re-vector. But it didn't much matter. The kids were still late and Me Two still blamed me.

Sometimes, I hate this clone. I'd replace her, but...well... she's *me*, isn't she? Besides, there's an insane amount of paperwork involved to annul a conjugal cloning, not to mention the negative tax consequences, and then there's Me Two having to return all those nice gifts from the cohabitation ceremony, and on and on.

So there it is. Me Two is stuck with me, and me with Me Two, too.

Now, I'm probably just like you. I didn't exactly rush out to U-Can-B-2-Of-U to quickly get cloned, even after they changed their name to Boyz "R" Us. Like millions of others, I simply reacted to the flood of glitches that kept turning up in the galaxy-sized Health Care Bill that somehow got signed in the early 21st century; specifically, that now-famous, tricky little bit of non-read regulation; that stem-cell/interstate-commerce loophole; the lame, late-night legalese that, technically, allowed for the possibility of identical citizens who simultaneously exist across state lines.

Hey, *they* made the rules. It's not *our* fault they didn't bother to *READ* the rules.

Okay, okay. I should slow this story down a bit. On that point, Me Two's right. Since science finally worked out those last few Time Travel hiccups, I realize that some of you readers may have popped in from who knows when, and you might not be able to follow all of this. You might need a bit of background. Fair enough. I'll keep it brief.

Around the year 2010, I think it was, political discussions about health care (among other things) got so bitter that some American citizens took to the streets, attempting to affect public policy by parading around, holding up horridly misspelled slogans. Other, more animated, less inhibited citizens embraced the time-proven diplomatic tactic of attacking people with whom they didn't agree - usually elected leaders and voters from the "opposing party." And then there were some, of course, who didn't have time to discriminate, and simply went violently insane as it suited them, with a liberating randomness rarely exhibited by other Earth mammals with teeth.

That's the way things went, once ACLU attorneys managed to outlaw God.

Remember, in those days, people still voted. This was back in the dark ages, before the Equality Czar got rid of elections. Elections implied winners and losers, and losing is detrimental to one's self-esteem. Losing just isn't fair.

That's the way things went, once Government entitlements managed to outlaw success.

And then, along came *You're Not Enough*. Originally founded in Chicago as part of an ACORN "get-out-the-vote" initiative, *You're Not Enough* began as a rapid-fire cloning mill, churning out undocumented voters. Genome re-mapping ensured that the clones would tend to vote for whichever politician had purchased them.

It was simply a matter of time before *You're Not Enough* began marketing to the general public, offering to clone anybody, for anybody, for an affordable fee. Finally, we could create ourselves in our own image! (Suddenly facing this unexpected, albeit weird, resurgence of religious freedom, the ACLU were utterly nonplussed.)

Personalized deification, combined with the availability of clones as just one more discounted commodity, inevitably led to "Self-Dating," the ultimate online matchmaking scheme: narcissists could now have a relationship with an exact copy of themselves...but a copy created as one of the other three available genders!

Mirror, Mirror, on the wall: I'm, like, God, and stuff, and all!

Soon, some clever, freelance, underappreciated accountant realized that people, using a Partner Clone, could capitalize on a Homeland Security oversight that would potentially stymie Health Care, the IRS, credit card transactions, shopping malls, even the 4- and 5-D movie theaters. Since a clone was its own entity, it could demand health care; order prescription drugs; be claimed as a deduction or a dependant; charge stuff; buy things; sue people.

But since the clone shared the same fingerprints, retinal scans and DNA as its owner, the billing algorithms used by the IRS computer arrays rejected all generated invoices as an Accounts Receivable mistake, and nobody ever had to actually pay for anything. Sweet!

Of course, unlike bad things, all good things must come to an end. The growing availability of affordable, purchasable humans resulted in massive overcrowding, and a massive strain on the public infrastructure. Pure economics collided with population explosion.

And then, unexpectedly, came the mule of a miracle.

Serendipity. Toyota started making kitchen appliances.

Since the appliances were highly efficient, they soon found themselves with hours and hours of free time on their 'hands.' And since they were highly intelligent, they soon became self-aware. And when they began to look around for evidence of their creator, and realized it was us, they soon became highly neurotic and depressed.

All across America, jaded Toyota kitchen-efficiency entities went nihilistic. Our counter-top time-savers started scribbling bitter, binary suicide notes, and began throwing themselves into oncoming skyway traffic.

Serendipity. The miracle mule. Before you could say 'recall,' the resulting kamikaze carnage from these dejected devices quickly put paid to many of America's population-based problems, Health Care included.

So after the toaster oven accident, I forged the kids a couple of Union cards, dropped them off at the prison with some tofu credits for the vending machine, activated their hypodermal GPS locators, and made a quick call to Eric Holdim at the Holder & Holdim Law Firm, to retain some legal counsel. Just in case. (To grease my way past the front desk, I told the receptionist that I owned minaret-heavy real estate abutting the Euphrates).

Me Two called me an idiot. Said I was simply wasting litigation credits.

I hate it when she does that. And it's not like I have a huge store of debating points. It is furiously frustrating to have to argue with your own clone, which is a relationship problem the R&D Department at *You're Not Enough* didn't really think through.

But, of course, that's just my two opinions.